PEAK
PERFORMANCE

PEAK PERFORMANCE

Mental Training Techniques
of the World's Greatest Athletes

Charles A. Garfield, Ph.D.,
with Hal Zina Bennett

JEREMY P. TARCHER, INC.
Los Angeles
Distributed by Houghton Mifflin Company
Boston

Library of Congress Cataloging in Publication Data

Garfield, Charles A.
  Peak performance.

  Bibliography: p. 207
  Includes index.
  1. Sports—Psychological aspects. 2. Athletes—
Training of. I. Bennett, Hal Zina, 1936–
II. Title.
GV706.4.G37 1984   796'.01   84–71
ISBN 0–87477–214–1

Requests for such permissions should be addressed to:

Jeremy P. Tarcher, Inc.
9110 Sunset Blvd.
Los Angeles, CA 90069

Design by Tanya Maiboroda

MANUFACTURED IN THE UNITED STATES OF AMERICA

S 10 9 8 7 6 5 4 3 2 1

First Edition

To Bill Pearl

Friend, bodybuilder supreme, and mentor to three generations of weight-trained athletes.

Thanks, "Big Medicine," for proving to thousands of us that an unyielding commitment to excellence and an unfailing support of other people are what constitute the true peak performer.

Acknowledgments

As with virtually all attempts at creation, this book was a collective act. Special thanks must be offered to:

Al Oerter, four-time Olympic gold medalist in the discus, an Olympic contender at age 48, and one of history's truly great athletes. During a dozen or so joint weight-training sessions before the 1968 Olympic Games, I saw in Al a mental toughness and determination I had never before encountered. Along with some of our peak performing Apollo colleagues at Grumman Aerospace Corporation, Al provided me with a magnificent prototype of the peak performer.

Marilyn King, my training partner *and* two-time member of the U.S. Olympic team in the Pentathlon, whose committed friendship helped me test many of the ideas in the best of laboratories, the gym.

Ben and Joe Weider, international leaders in disseminating sports-training information. With appreciation for their wholehearted support of my research and ideas on peak performance.

Enrico Jones, professor of psychology at the University of California, Berkeley, and one of America's most insightful psychologists. Our dozen years of working out together have contributed considerably to my understanding of the tremendous impact of the mind on physical functioning.

Cindy Spring, special partner and committed recreational athlete, for her integrity and concern for the life-affirming values underlying our peak performance theories and practices.

My parents, Sylvia and Ed Garfield, for their invaluable contribution—the need for and love of a powerful commitment to a compelling mission.

World-class and recreational athletes, coaches, and training partners too numerous to mention who continue to give the best of themselves in our growing understanding of athletic genius and peak performance in all walks of life.

Charles A. Garfield, Ph.D.

I would especially like to thank Susan Sparrow and Linda Greer French for their editorial support. Thanks also to Derek Gallagher, Mary Nadler, and B. Wallace Hood, Jr., for their professional attention to the book.

Hal Zina Bennett

Contents

PEAK
PERFORMANCE

PEAK PERFORMANCE TRAINING

An Overview of

the Program

Most athletes will acknowledge that 60 to 90 percent of success in sports is due to mental factors and psychological mastery. In spite of this fact, we rarely encounter either recreational or competitive athletes who regularly practice disciplined, scientifically based mental training programs. Sensing the importance of mental training in recent years, athletes and coaches have experimented, usually on a hit-or-miss basis, with a confusing array of techniques. Too often these techniques have been orphaned fragments from larger programs, and, taken out of context, have led to disillusionment about the whole notion of mental training. In addition, athletes and their coaches, perhaps seeking the proverbial "silver bullet," have had unrealistic or simplistic views of how these techniques should be practiced. They have expected miracles from small investments. It has always seemed ironic to me that many of the athletes who had such great expectations for mental training—expecting somehow to leap tall buildings with a single bound after a few sessions of relaxation or visualization—were the same ones who were capable of, and knew the necessity for, solid, programmed physical training.

We know that some of the early failures in mental training for athletes have been due to the lack of a comprehensive, structured program. Until now, we have not invested the time and energy required to raise mental training to a level of sophistication at least equal to that of the physical training programs available to the serious athlete.

My mission in *Peak Performance* has been to synthesize the best sports research conducted in the United States, the U.S.S.R., East Germany, and elsewhere into a results-oriented *program*, one that is both comprehensive and flexible, providing equal assistance to the competitive and the serious recreational athlete in search of peak performance.

The Peak Performance Training Program, which you find here in this book, consists of six key lessons in mental training. These lessons are divided into learning phases, with each one taking from ten to thirty minutes per day. For this reason, as you read through these pages, you will see many small exercises rather than a few large ones.

Most people are accustomed to being presented with a single, large learning task that requires weeks and sometimes months of tedious repetition before improvement can be noticed. While certain kinds of athletes may reap benefits from this common training approach, the stress and frustration often experienced with it can actually work against many of the central principles of Peak Performance Training.

It is vital in Peak Performance Training that athletes experience immediate feedback for their efforts wherever possible and that there be a high probability for success in each learning phase. The immediate feedback for each phase may come in any number of ways, but it is most effective when experienced on a deeply personal level. The feedback may be in the form of an improvement in physical performance, or through the grasping of a method to improve one's mental control, or as self-discovery, or as an increased understanding about the human mechanisms that contribute to optimal performance.

The Peak Performance Training Program has been carefully orchestrated to balance the performance of tasks with the enjoyment of feedback in order to maintain a high level of interest and motivation throughout. One mechanism we have employed to make this possible is the designing of each training phase in such a way that the benefits will not be limited to the sports arena, but will apply to all aspects of a person's life. Indeed, parts of the Peak Performance Training Program, such as the work in Lesson 1, on volition, have helped people make more effective choices in their personal lives, and the material on relaxation in Lesson 3 has carried over into people's work lives, as a stress reduction technique minimizing illness and maximizing productivity.

My choice of exercises in the Peak Performance Training Program that would broaden and enhance performance abilities outside athletics was a deliberate one. At Performance Sciences Institute, in Berkeley, California, where much of my research has been done, I saw that by providing skills with a variety of applications, practice toward the mastery of those skills would automatically take place during most of our waking hours. Thus, learning would be more rapid and more complete.

Because the Peak Performance Training Program does carry over into many of your daily activities, you'll notice your performance will be enhanced in everything you do. For this reason it is important to recognize the truth in a statement made by one of the athletes with whom I have worked: "Excellence is never limited to the playing field. Of necessity, it becomes a way of life."

Over the past several years, in my capacity as a lecturer and consultant on peak performance for many of our nation's most prestigious corporations, I have been struck by the power of sports as a metaphorical proving ground for executives. The same techniques used by athletes to achieve peak performance in sports are being applied in the highly competitive world of business. Indeed, significant numbers of our nation's top executives take their participation in sports very seriously, going beyond the issue of fitness, which may have attracted them to athletics in the first place. Like many of Japan's industrial leaders, who have long included techniques of the martial arts in their leadership training, many American businessmen have discovered that athletics can serve as a laboratory for putting to the test and perfecting, in a deeply personalized way, such skills as goal-setting and visualization. These two areas have already proved themselves to be at least as important in the corporate world as they are in the athletic world.

Because of the growing awareness of the role that athletic training can play in the corporate world, I predict a time when every company that hopes to compete in today's marketplace will have a gym of its own and will schedule gym time for all top managers and executives. Such plans will not be seen as frills but as necessities for the survival of the corporation itself. Undoubtedly, an important part of the sports program in each of these gyms will be a training component that spells out in detail how the skills being learned and tested in the gym can be applied by the individual to better perform his or her role in the corporation.

WHAT YOU NEED TO KNOW ABOUT THE EXERCISES IN THIS BOOK

Following the first chapter, "Soviet Shamans in Milan," you will find six lessons representing the complete Peak Performance Training Program. Each lesson contains exercises, called phases, and evaluative material, as well as text discussing the purpose and the scientific background of these exercises and examples that establish their importance to the athlete. The complete Peak Performance Training Program is designed for committed competitive athletes. For recreational athletes who do not have the time to invest in the complete Peak Performance Training Program I have designed a short course. The eight exercises required for the short course are indicated below by asterisks.

At the end of each lesson you will find a section called Applications for this Lesson Outside Sports. In these sections there are suggestions for some of the ways you might use your new skills in your professional and personal life. Integrating your peak performance skills into these nonathletic areas accomplishes two things. First, it increases the opportunities to practice, and thus master, these new skills, and second, it makes peak performance a way of life, increasing your productivity, your potential for success, and your sense of personal well-being in everything you do. Here is an outline of the lessons and their learning phases:

Lesson 1 Sports Motivation Analysis
Discovering the You Who Can Become a Peak
Performer
Identifying Your Volition* 30 min x 3
Evaluating Your Volition 15 min x1
The Goal Profile 30 min x 1

Lesson 2 Unveiling Your Mission
Goal-setting Techniques for Fully Actualizing **Your**
Athletic Ambitions
Mission Statement* 30 min x 1
Long-term Goal Statement 15 min x 1
The Peak Performance Assessment Chart 30 min x 1
The Program Training Plan varied (app 45 min 1 hr x 1
Translating Goals into Mental Images 30 min x 1

Lesson 3 Voluntary Relaxation
Developing the Primary Skill for Controlling
Concentration and Physical Intensity
p 107 Exploring Relaxation and Tension* 20 min x 1 (for short deep Relax
p 110 Breathing for Peak Performance 20 min 13 .0
p 114 Autogenic Training* 15 min/twice a day for 3 months

Lesson 4 Mental Rehearsal
Using the Powers of the Mind to Perfect **Your**
Performance
Seeing with the Mind's Eye* 20 min x 1
Your Best Performance and Beyond 20 min x 3
Directing the Movies of Mental Imagery* 30 min x 3

Lesson 5   Athletic Poise
Maintaining Peak Performance Feelings
The Peak Performance Scale   *30m × 1*
Creating an Expectation of Success* *20m × 1*

Lesson 6   Letting Go
Turning over the Controls to Your Internal Peak
Performer
Letting Go*   *20m — before performy*

The lessons are presented consecutively, and *it is necessary to complete all the work in one lesson before going on to the next.* In most cases, each succeeding lesson depends on your mastering the skills from the preceding lesson or lessons. The skill learned in the final lesson, Letting Go, will serve to orchestrate all the skills that you learned before it. In a very real sense, this final skill is the focal point of everything contained in the book.

The time required to develop all the skills presented in this program will depend on many factors. But, if you work regularly, three to four times each week, incorporating these mental exercises with an effective physical training program, you will notice subtle improvements in your performance almost immediately. More dramatic changes will occur in two to three months as you develop a firm grasp of the complete set of skills.

It is advised that throughout the program you respect your own pace, proceeding only as rapidly as you find comfortable and enjoyable. In the beginning, especially, it may take several attempts before you feel the benefits of a particular exercise. Do not take this as a sign that the exercise doesn't work or, more important, that you are for some reason not learning it. What you are doing is beginning a training process requiring a period of growth. You will actually be undergoing physiological changes, the same way as you would in physical training. As you master new skills, you will find the exercises becoming automatic, and as this occurs you'll experience increased improvement in your athletic performance.

Allow yourself time not only to master each skill, but also to enjoy the numerous ways in which you can utilize that skill in your life. When faced with difficult choices in your personal life, make use of what you have learned in Lesson 1 to help solve those problems. When you encounter challenges in the workplace, make use of the goal-setting skills you have acquired in Lesson 2. When tension builds in any area of your life, apply what you have learned in the lessons on relaxation.

As with any mental training program, make certain that all exercises are practiced only in a safe, comfortable, environment. I recommend designating a particularly quiet room as a mental training sanctuary.

Quality, not quantity, is the guiding principle here. Focus on the benefits you derive along the way, rather than on how many lessons you have completed or on how many you have yet to do. The program is designed so that improvement will be experienced at every step along the path; you don't have to wait until the end, when you've mastered every lesson, to reap the pleasures of your investment of time and energy.

I strongly recommend that you keep a loose-leaf binder for making notes on evaluative material and for keeping a record of your progress. The program itself requires some specific written work.

In addition, you will find it helpful, especially in Lessons 3, 4, and 5 to have a friend read the instructions aloud as you do each exercise. The reasons will become obvious in the relaxation exercises, where a particular state of consciousness is induced that can easily be disturbed by your having to go back and read instructions. If a second person is not available, prerecord the exercises from the book on a tape and play it back to yourself.

Whether making your own recordings or having the exercises read by a friend, you should follow certain rules for best results:

1. Speak slowly and clearly.
2. Speak in a soothing voice, keeping consonants soft, and linger over vowels to emphasize the soothing quality.

3. Pause between each step of instruction, allowing time to accomplish the objective. This may require experimentation on your part, but a pause of three seconds will generally provide enough time to fulfill the instruction without your losing your attention.

You will notice, especially as you read the relaxation exercises in Lesson 3, that most sentences are generally simple in structure and that repetition occurs from line to line. *Do not confuse simplicity of communication with simplemindedness!* Although by conversational standards it is monotonous, this style of presentation is deliberate and necessary and follows the tenets of Johannes Schultz, a neurologist and psychiatrist whose work is the basis for most systems of autosuggestion (biofeedback, Autogenic Training, and others), and of the Russian physician A. G. Odessky, whose work will be discussed throughout this book. The entire style of presentation is designed to guide your mind, particularly your subconscious mind, while you are in a deeply relaxed state, a state of consciousness that would be disrupted by a more active delivery style.

Although the practice and discipline required in this program represents a good deal of hard work, I guarantee encouraging signs of growth and increased motivation along the way. Each of these signs—be they reducing pregame nervousness, cutting seconds from your running time, or improving your tennis serve—will be a reward as well as an incentive. Each skill you acquire will become an integral part of your repetoire, allowing you to be a peak performer more regularly. Everything you learn in this program will motivate you to obtain a higher level of performance in your sport.

Bear in mind as you begin this program that our singular aim here is *mental* training. Although mental training greatly enhances physical training, it does not supplant it. All athletic training programs must include a balance of physical and mental training and nutrition. There are a great many books available for physical training and nutrition, books you may obtain at your local bookstore or library.

As you begin your work in Peak Performance Training, consider this vital conclusion of Olympic gold medalist Bruce Jenner: "I always felt that my greatest asset was not my physical ability, it was my mental ability." The same sentiment has been expressed by other superathletes, from Jack Nicklaus to Bruce Lee to Pele to Billie Jean King. Given their record of achievement, you can be sure that this principle will help you in developing your optimal athletic potential.

SOVIET SHAMANS IN MILAN

Discovering the Mental Training Techniques of the World's Greatest Athletes

> **The shaping of psychological readiness is one of the main tasks in preparing athletes for competitions.**
>
> V. A. Romanov
> sports psychologist

It is now history that in the 1976 Olympics the Russians won more gold medals than did any other country. Their victories also included two of the three judo titles ordinarily taken by the Japanese. The East German team placed second, its women swimmers taking eleven of the thirteen medals. The United States placed third.

The athletic achievements of the Russian and East German teams were so extraordinary that the use of steroids or other prohibited drugs was widely suspected. Adding to this speculation was the fact that a Bulgarian weight lifter lost his Olympic medal after laboratory tests revealed traces of steroids in his urine. Kurt Tittel, director of the Leipzig Institute of Sports in East Germany (a remarkable fourteen-acre sports laboratory employing 900 people, half of them scientists), vehemently denied allegations of drug use and claimed that new training methods alone were responsible for the impressive victories.

The controversy polarized the athletic community. Many people continued to believe that drugs contributed to the Soviets' success; others believed that Tittel was telling the truth and that the revolutionary training techniques developed by the Russians were soon to be revealed to the rest of the world.

Slowly, motivated in part by the desire of the countries in question to defend their honor, the truth began to trickle out from behind the Iron Curtain. In November 1976, *Track and Field News* reported that "mental training sessions" were being employed by the Soviet weight lifters. Still shrouded in mystery, this news was merely a glimpse of things to come.

From the outset, politics has played an important role in motivating the communist countries to develop high-level sports programs. For example, East Germany had been shunned by many countries, including the United States, which had once refused to grant visas allowing East German athletes to compete in America. By 1976, after having won 92 Olympic gold medals, 263 European titles, and 340 world titles using the new athletic training methods, East Germany found new diplomatic doors being opened.

THE EXTENT OF SOVIET INVESTMENT IN SPORTS

In 1979, while lecturing in Milan, I met a group of Soviet sports psychologists and physiologists who thoroughly challenged my perception of athletic training. Their innovative approach to training was revolutionary, suggesting the need for a complete reassessment of Western sports philosophy.

I spent several days with the Soviets, during which time we exchanged notes about training superathletes. Many years prior to that, I had launched a research project of my own back in the States in which I was collecting interviews with peak performers from all walks of life. At Performance Sciences Institute, I had been trying to determine the skills and characteristics shared in common by extraordinary performers in athletics, academics, business, science, and the arts. The Soviets were intrigued by my findings, but, as it turned out, what they offered in return seemed light-years ahead.

My Soviet hosts explained that in East Germany there are sixteen government-sponsored sports schools, where students receive fourteen hours of athletic training per week in addition to the regular academic curriculum. Athletes with potential for world-class competition are identified in grade school and are assigned to the best trainers. In East Germany, 60 percent of the population engages regularly and rigorously in some form of athletic activity, be it in recreational sports or in more serious competition, and approximately 2 percent of the gross national product is invested in athletic programs.

An even more impressive scenario was described for Russia. Astronomical sums of money are poured into athletics, much of it donated by labor unions, consumer co-ops, government agencies, and sports societies. There are reportedly 5 million athletes in Russia, and 6,000 sports schools, 57,000 gymnasiums, and 220,000 sports clubs. In addition, there are thousands of tracks, pools, tennis courts, ski centers, and stadiums—all available for public use.

Every four years in Moscow, 10,000 Soviet athletes, the cream of the crop from the sports schools, participate in the Spartakiad, a national rehearsal for the Olympics. This celebration of youthful athletic accomplishment supports and dramatically demonstrates the high value placed on athletic achievement, establishing clear-cut incentives for both parents and children.

The extensive investment in athletic research in the communist countries began early in the 1950s as part of the Soviet space program. Alexander Romen's basic research, which eventually led to programs for teaching optimal sports performance, explored the possibility of employing ancient yogic techniques to teach cosmonauts to control psychophysiological processes while in space. This field of inquiry came to be known as "self-regulation training" or "psychic self-regulation." It focused on the learning of methods for voluntarily controlling bodily functions such as heart rate, temperature, and muscle tension as well as emotional reactions to such stressful situations as zero gravity.

Prior to this, most physiologists had believed these functions to be largely outside our conscious control. Romen and others proved that humans *can* control the so-called autonomic functions, allowing them to raise or lower their heart rates, temperature, excitement levels, and so on. These researchers also developed methods for teaching control techniques that did not require the use of laboratory paraphernalia, such as that used in biofeedback training, but that depended instead on signals from the subject's own body and mind. However, nearly twenty years passed before these methods were applied in the Soviet and East German sports programs.

SOVIET PERCEPTIONS OF COMPETITION

The Soviets perceive athletics as a potent form of individual expression. This is poignantly reflected in their revisions of the meaning of competition. Soviet youth are taught to look upon competition not only as an opportunity to prove oneself better than others, but as the ultimate motivation for developing the best in oneself. One is taught to look upon competitors as equals. When you compete with an equal and wish to excel, you are forced to draw upon resources usually considered to be outside the normal range of capabilities. Through this effort you become more fully *self-actualized*, a term I heard repeatedly from the Soviets I met in Milan. Understanding this shift in defining competition is necessary in order to appreciate the philosophy from which the Soviet training programs were developed.

Polish psychologist Tadeusz Rychta has said: "Sport training, through its physical actions, activates those human sources that develop an athlete's personality, improve physical and psychological skills, and discover unlimited possibilities of human mind and body. Performance is only a means to facilitate the athlete's self-actualization, to help athletes create in hard work undisputable cultural values of modern humanity."

THE ROLE OF SPORTS PSYCHOLOGISTS IN THE SOVIET UNION

In the Iron Curtain countries, sports psychologists are central figures in facilitating the athlete's quest for optimal performance. They have quite a different place in society than do their counterparts in the United States. Whereas the sports psychologist in this country may be perceived as a person who helps the athlete correct problems, the sports psychologist in the Soviet Union assumes an active role at the very beginning of all training regimens, concentrating on creating methods to maximize performance.

Russian sports psychologists have been so highly esteemed that at least one has been awarded the venerated title of Academician, which elevates the recipient to the level of a national hero. The Russian public regards the Academician in much the same way that Americans regard an exceptional athlete or a war hero.

FROM HOLOCAUST SURVIVORS TO SUPERATHLETES

Although specific skills were first directly applied in the Soviet space program, the Russians' interest in peak performance began with their study of Holocaust survivors of World War II. They observed that these survivors, in spite of the most heinous treatment by their captors, possessed an ability to tap into *hidden reserves,* to find renewed strength to go on. This affirmation of the potential of hidden reserves prompted Russian researchers to begin probing the mental and physical characteristics not only of these survivors but also of high achievers, such as athletes, musicians, dancers, and artists. There was a common trait in all of them, an ability to extend themselves far beyond the capabilities of the average person.

It is ironic that out of some of the most violently dehumanizing experiences in history emerged a field of scientific inquiry having potential for leading humanity to its highest levels of achievement. If the Soviet claims were true, they had developed programs to facilitate evolution by helping people realize far more of their potentials in athletics, the arts, and science. That the starting point for all this would have been the unspeakable suffering of millions gives this new science an heroic dimension akin to the phoenix rising from the flames.

In my meetings with the Soviet researchers in Milan, they discussed government-funded athletic programs that integrate sophisticated mental training and rigorous physical training. One study evaluating these intensive programs suggests their potential. Four matched groups of world-class Soviet athletes diligently trained for many hours each week. The training regimens were as follows:

Group I—100 percent physical training

Group II—75 percent physical training, 25 percent mental training

Group III—50 percent physical training, 50 percent mental training

Group IV—25 percent physical training, 75 percent mental training

When the four groups were compared shortly before the 1980 Winter Games in Lake Placid, Group IV had shown significantly greater improvement than Group III, with Groups II and I following, in that order.

The Soviet researchers had a name for their new system of training and study, but it is almost impossible to find an adequate translation. Terms such as *psychophysical, psycho-*

kinetic, and *psychosomatic,* while implying a state of mind and body working together, somehow seem inadequate. The closest we have come is *anthropomaximology,* a tongue twister for which I am quite happy to substitute "the study and practice of peak performance."

FROM THEORY TO PRACTICE

After spending a number of days with the Soviet researchers I had heard enough theory; I wanted to see results. Following a formal social function at the villa of the mayor of Milan that ended around midnight, we found ourselves roaming around the streets of Milan, fired by our enthusiasm and seeking a gym with a good set of weights. This midnight search seemed preposterous to me, but my Soviet companions acted as though it was quite normal.

Although Milan is a large cosmopolitan city there was little chance of finding a gym open at this late hour. Undaunted, my Soviet friends insisted upon returning to the mayor's villa, where they unabashedly roused the mayor and told him what we needed. Given the time and the intense expressions on the faces of the Soviet scientists, the mayor apparently decided this unusual request must be important, deserving his official attention. After being on the phone for what to us seemed like an hour, he returned to announce that he had arranged to put the best gym in Milan at our disposal.

It was well past 2 A.M. when we assembled at the gym. My Soviet friends, looking grave and deliberate in their now rumpled formal attire, opened attaché cases they had brought from their hotel. They produced a portable EEG for measuring brainwaves, an ECG for measuring cardiac activity, an EMG for measuring muscular activity, and more. I was soon hooked up to all this paraphernalia while my associates took notes and made various computations.

The Soviets asked whether I was currently in competition or working out with any degree of regularity. I told them that I was not in competition and that I had not been in a gym for a number of months. It had been more than eight years since I'd been in serious training and bench-pressed 365 pounds. With my casual workouts in recent years, I seldom, if ever, lifted more than 275 or 280 pounds.

The Soviets were interested in the fact that I had once bench-pressed 365 pounds, and they wanted to know how long I thought it might take to get into shape to lift at that level again. I assured them I could do it within nine to twelve months. After several minutes of consultation, they asked what I thought would be the absolute maximum I could lift right now. I said I was willing to try for a 300-pound lift, but I warned them that I had not made such a lift in years. They urged me to try, saying it was an essential element in their demonstration.

With enormous difficulty, and due mostly to the excitement of the situation, I managed to lift the 300 pounds—much to my own surprise. Following the lift, the Soviets went to work measuring my height, weight, percentage of body fat, and metabolic rate, and even took a blood sample. They worked over me in silence, reading meters, computing, and assessing the information registering on their instruments. At last they seemed satisfied with their tabulations and went to the next step of their demonstration.

They asked me to lie on my back and proceeded to guide me into a deep state of relaxation. I was fully awake and alert, aware of everything going on around me. Yet every muscle in my body relaxed, and I felt more at ease than ever before in my life. They asked me to imagine my arms and legs becoming increasingly heavy and warm. A warm, tingling sensation spread over me.

When nearly forty minutes had passed, they asked me to sit up slowly. They told me to stare at the weight I was going to lift. Meanwhile, 65 pounds had been added to the 300 I'd barely wrestled off my chest earlier.

Next, I was told to mentally visualize myself approaching the bar, sitting on the bench, lying down, and then, with total confidence, lifting the 365 pounds. I was also instructed to imagine the sounds I would hear, the dull metallic ring as the bar tipped slightly, jangling the weights together, the sound of my own breathing, and any vocalizing I ordinarily did when working out.

Suddenly, I became apprehensive. I sensed they were actually anticipating that I would rally my forces and lift the 365-pound bar. I was certain I couldn't do it. I knew my limits. And considering the circumstances, I'd be lucky to lift 300 pounds again.

The needles on the monitors clearly revealed my anxiety. But my associates urged me on and again encouraged me to visualize myself clearly and confidently lifting the 365-pound bar. They asked me to zoom in and out on the images imprinted in my mind, to view myself from above and the side, to look closely at my hands grasping the bar, to imagine how my muscles would feel as I completed the lift. They talked me through the entire process again and again, all the while monitoring my mental and physical responses with their instruments.

Surprisingly, everything began to come together for me, much the way it does split seconds before you know you are going to succeed at an athletic goal for which you have been preparing for months. The imagery now imprinted in my mind began to guide my physical movements. Slowly and patiently, their voices sure yet gentle, the Soviets led me through the lift. I became convinced I could do it. The world around me seemed to fade, giving way to self-confidence, belief in myself, and then to deliberate action.

I lifted the weight!

I was absolutely astounded. Filled with the exhilaration of triumph, I wanted to go on. I felt ready to challenge the world record, but more rational minds prevailed.

"We calculate your present capabilities at somewhere between 345 and 395," I was told. "We chose 365 as a midway point. You no doubt could do more, maybe 395, but there are present physical limits that should be respected. You could tear a muscle or tendon. It doesn't make sense to chance it."

My mind buzzed as I returned to my hotel. I went to bed but couldn't sleep. It was so overwhelmingly exciting to make, as though by magic, a lift that should have been impossible. And what excited me more than my lift was the realization that the Soviets had developed a system for tapping apparently hidden reserves in a dependable, scientificaily proven manner.

If I were to believe in what had happened at the gym, I had to revise my thinking substantially about the process of athletic training and performance. It was not what the ancients had thought, that accessing hidden reserves and achieving optimal performance was a "gift of the gods"—a concept that puts peak performance outside our conscious control. The Soviets had demonstrated that optimal human performance could be *orchestrated.*

In searching for clues as to how this orchestration could occur, I was reminded of my experiences in the Apollo space program. In the early phases of research, scientists pointed out that during prolonged lunar spaceflights, astronauts would undergo mental and physical changes that would include irregularity of blood pressure and heart rate, enlargement of the heart, decreased peripheral blood flow, and numerous psychological changes. At first our physicians on the space program considered using drugs to combat these effects, but since these had never been tested under zero gravity, the prospect seemed too risky. Alternatives were sought, and one group of medical researchers began to explore self-regulation through meditation and biofeedback. The title of the project was Neurophysiological Autoregulation During Prolonged Spaceflight. These researchers suggested not only that the brain could be imprinted with an image of a physical event *before* the act had actually been accomplished, but also that once an image had been clearly imprinted the actual physical event could be far more easily executed even though the slow, gradual physical process ordinarily associated with training had been largely left out.

Part of the astronauts' training at NASA included hours in a spaceflight simulator that put them through the physiological and psychological stress of lift-off and the weightlessness of spaceflight. During simulation training, the astronauts received signals that required them to respond to hundreds of emergency events.

The simulator literally taught the astronauts how to pre-program their minds and bodies to accomplish tasks in a situation no human had ever been in before. The preprogramming subsequently proved effective in actual spaceflight; the astronauts were able to perform "new" operations extremely well when challenged in space.

In everyday life we depend on *feedback* to program our nervous systems. However, the simulator was, in effect, *feeding forward*. This meant that the nervous system of any astronaut trained in the flight simulator could be educated *before* the fact, so that when the real physical event took place the astronaut would respond appropriately.

Even if *feed forward* was possible, this did not explain how muscles could become stronger in such a short period of time. Although I had at one time in my life lifted 365 pounds, it did not seem to be a possibility that night in Milan. Logically, muscles just couldn't work that way. Yet I had done it.

After returning to the United States, I continued to look for explanations for what I had experienced in Milan. In the beginning, I was startled to discover broad overlaps between the work of the Russians and of our own psychologists. For example, there is now not a shadow of a doubt in my mind that the Soviets have long been aware of the work of the American psychologist Abraham Maslow and of his exploration of what he called "peak experiences" and the emotional foundations that accompany such moments. Similarly, in the work of leading Soviet researchers such as Alexander Romen and A. G. Odessky quite open allusions are made to the work of Edmund Jacobsen (Progressive Relaxation) and Johannes Schulz and Wolfgang Luthe (Autogenic Training). In conversations with the Soviet researchers in Milan, I had also learned that they were aware of the work of Elmer and Alyce Green (*Beyond Biofeedback*, 1977), who, with the help of a grant from the Menninger Foundation in 1964, studied the effects of the mind on the so-called autonomic functions—including the study of muscular and hormonal changes applicable to sports.

As these areas of overlap became more obvious, I discovered that far from lacking scientific foundations for peak performance training, American and European scientific libraries were probably even more complete than were the Soviets'. I now believe that Western research has contributed significantly to mental training programs so brilliantly developed by the Soviet and East German sports academies. It is even more ironic that so many of our own coaches and athletes have, until quite recently, been resistant to systematic mental training, training that is as homespun as baseball.

I do not mean to imply that we should take credit for the Soviets' mental training techniques; on the contrary! It has been, after all, the Soviets, not us, who had the foresight and ingenuity to develop mental training techniques from what was considered in our country a rather obscure field of scientific inquiry.

Yet the mental training of athletes is truly an international creation. As in many areas of science and technology—from acupuncture to atomic energy—the discoveries of one scientist are quickly disseminated to every corner of the globe. At times, certain ideas seem to travel with special rapidity, making their impact a global rather than a regional or national one. It is clear that mental training for the athlete is emerging as a significant area of interest worldwide.

THE UNEXPECTEDNESS OF PEAK PERFORMANCE

Through my own research in peak performance, I have found a common denominator among men and women engaged in a variety of activities. It was the ability to reach into themselves and draw upon sources of energy and inspiration that usually transcend everyday life—the hidden reserves. Again and again, athletes said that they made major leaps of improvement in their performances when these hidden reserves were accessed. Such moments were often described as "unexpected" and "awesome." Sportswriter and runner Valerie Andrews stated in her book, *The Psychic Power of Running*: "As we begin to approach our optimum level of fitness, we may experience startling transformations of the body and mind, with major advances in both athletic capabilities and consciousness occurring all at once."

In the process of looking for explanations, I ran across William James's essay "The Energies of Man," in which he wrote: "If an unusual necessity forces us to press outward, a surprising thing occurs. The fatigue gets worse up to a certain critical point, when gradually or suddenly it passes away and we are fresher than before. We have evidently tapped a new level of energy, masked until then by the fatigue-obstacle usually obeyed. There may be layer after layer of this experience. A third and fourth 'wind' may supervene."

On an energy level, peak performers often speak of a very high or ecstatic experience. Mike Mentzer described his workouts in preparing for the Mr. Olympia competition, the world's most prestigious bodybuilding event, in the following way: "I'd feel the rush of vital energy *streaming* through my body, causing me at times to break out into a long belly laugh which I had to stifle for fear of appearing maniacal."

I found that the literature of extraordinary sports accomplishment is in fact full of such quotes, but I had no idea how they related to the most recent experiments in the physiology of exercise. To my knowledge the research in sports science had not yet addressed this aspect of the upper limits of performance.

A NEW MARRIAGE OF SCIENCE AND ATHLETICS

The mental training I had experienced in Milan emphasized deep relaxation and the powerful imagining of myself making the lift. How could this affect my physical performance? How did it work in terms of our knowledge about the relationships between body and mind? I began to review the research literature on the neurophysiology of exercise. The most recent articles established that the mind and body are inseparable and that thoughts and feelings may affect every cell in our bodies. Medical and psychological research has demonstrated that mental states and attitudes can certainly make the difference between sickness and health. These are not just matters of cooperating or not cooperating with medical professionals who are offering treatment, but of thoughts and feelings actually enhancing or inhibiting healing processes within the body.

The pioneering work of medical researcher Hans Selye on stress established that vital functions such as blood flow and hormonal activity are dramatically influenced by our mental perceptions. Further research has shown that the balance of body fluids, the assimilation of minerals, and the transport of oxygen and carbon dioxide are all affected by our mental states. Since these are all essential elements in athletic performance, it is logical that mental conditioning should influence physical activity.

EMOTIONS AND SPECIFIC SIGNS AND SYMPTOMS

Triggered by thoughts and feelings, the brain can affect physical changes through three general routes: by transmitting impulses through the autonomic nervous system, by transmitting impulses through the brain's bulboreticular area to the muscles, and by regulation and control of certain endocrine glands.

Nearly all emotions can affect the autonomic nervous system. For example, excitement, such as anxiety, an intense competitive spirit, or rage, can cause a dramatic increase in arterial blood pressure, heart palpitations, and cold chills over the skin. Emotions such as worry, depression, or pregame jitters can have the opposite effect by slowing bodily functions and in extreme cases can cause anesthetization of the entire musculature. Sometimes excitation and worry occur simultaneously, causing violent physical reactions such as gastrointestinal distress, including vomiting and/or diarrhea.

Emotional stresses such as worry, anxiety, and self-doubt can be extremely detrimental in competition. Robbed of proper nutrients by the constricted blood flow caused by these emotions, the athlete's brain tends to focus on the last error or loss, rather than focusing on the goal at hand. Negative emotions of this kind have a hypnotic influence. The physical effects are felt almost instantly—and many athletes have not learned how to cope effectively with that level of self-hypnosis. Mental concentration can be vastly diminished, accompanied by a weakening of *volition* (the determination to win).

Most athletes know the physical signs and symptoms of negative emotions only too well: disrupted coordination, proneness to injury, shortness of breath, "choking," impaired vision, tearing eyes, cramped or knotted muscles, loss of flexibility, and even muscle fatigue.

According to Soviet research, all athletes experience at least some of these physical symptoms in the face of negative emotional stimulation. The Soviets' task became one of discovering what might be done to regulate such reactions at will, prior to their occurring in competition and regardless of the cause. In the process, the researchers discovered that mental training techniques not only combated negative reactions, but also threw open the doors to hidden reserves of energy and endurance.

In my own research with peak performers, I have found a number of behavior patterns and attitudes that are clearly related to the creation of positive mental states.

THE PEAK PERFORMANCE PROFILE

In his studies during the 1960s of "peak experiences"—mankind at its highest moments—Abraham Maslow reversed the traditional approach to examining problems of human behavior. Instead of scrutinizing dysfunction, Maslow focused on human behavior at its most elevating and personally satisfying levels. He found that during the peak experience his subjects had a sense of being more confident, *more fully integrated*, of having all their faculties, both mental and physical, of being totally tuned in to the moment. The integration of mental and physical aspects of human functioning contributed to a performance that was personally pleasurable and yet surpassed everyday expectations. Maslow wrote that during such moments, "the powers of the person come together in a particularly efficient and intensely enjoyable way, and in which he is more integrated and less split, more open for experience . . . more perfectly expressive or spontaneous, or fully functioning, more creative . . . more truly himself, more perfectly *actualizing* his potentialities . . . more fully human."

Echoing this notion of integration and self-power, most peak performers say that even when they enter a competitive event with an initial sense of nervousness, it gives way to a very clear *expectation* of success. This attitude was probably best demonstrated by Olympic gold medalist Bruce Jenner when he said, "I started to feel there was nothing I couldn't do if I had to. It was a feeling of awesome power, except that I was in awe of myself." More recently, I spoke with my training partner, Olympic pentathlete Marilyn King, who called her expectation of success a "kind of knowing that comes from inside, that whatever it is I choose to do, I can do it." Cindy Nelson, a member of the U.S. ski team, with a world championship silver medal and an Olympic bronze among her trophies, put it even more succinctly: "I know my place within myself."

Along with the expectation of success, peak performers say that *the everyday world recedes into the background* and that they have a feeling of being surrounded by an invisible envelope in which only the action they are engaging in seems to exist. At these times the athlete is so focused as to become largely unaware of himself. This is described by some as a form of amnesia, by others as a transcendence from usual habits of thought. Professional football player Jack Snow said, "If a plane crashed in the stadium, I don't think I'd notice it until the play was over."

Reports of this kind correspond with what Soviet sports psychologists tell us about peak performance: it is directed from deep within us, from an intuitive or subconscious level of our being, rather than being directed by our thoughts. At moments of peak performance the athlete is apparently released from conscious thought processes and goes on "automatic pilot," bringing major reserves to bear on the activity of the moment.

In the peak performance experience, the athlete focuses

on precisely the details of the play that allow him or her to respond optimally. There can be *intense focus on a small action,* isolated from the larger picture; Klaus DiBiasi, champion diver and three-time Olympic gold-medal winner was quoted in the book *Numero Uno*, by Bud and C. P. Greenspan, as saying, "You can remember each small amount of the dive." At the opposite pole, there can be *intense concentration on the big picture*, as noted by Bill Russell: "I could almost sense how the next play would develop and where the next shot would be taken. Even before the other team brought the ball in-bounds, I could feel it so keenly that I'd want to shout to my teammates, 'It's coming up there.' "

Many athletes have spoken of *a sense of power*, occurring at the apex of the peak performance that transcends their ordinary levels of energy and that seems to come from outside them. Basketball free-throw champion Patsy Neal described a "power present that allows the individual to 'walk on water,' to create miracles." What is even more interesting is that a surge of power is frequently apparent to teammates or other witnesses. After observing Peter Snell, a fellow runner said, "Snell took off so fast that it appeared like someone on a fast horse had lassoed him and jerked him ahead."

Again and again, athletes have described how at moments of peak performance they felt consumed by the momentum of the event itself, how the activity itself took over, and how they became perfectly synchronized within it. Some athletes said that they began to feel as though they were acting automatically, their minds and bodies like instruments perfectly tuned to the moment. They participated in the action without conscious thought.

In interviews throughout his career, boxer Ingemar Johansson insisted that his powerful right hand seemed to have a mind of its own, that when the time came to deliver the knockout punch he felt he surrendered to the action rather than taking an active part in it: "Without my telling it to, the right goes, and when it hits, there is this good feeling. . . . Something just right has been done."

The impressions athletes have of how they feel when immersed in an event in this way are interesting in themselves. Golfer Arnold Palmer has written: "I'd liken it to a sense of reverie—not a dreamlike state, but the somehow *insulated* state that a great musician achieves in a great performance."

Even professional football players, whom one would least expect to be attuned to subtle mental changes during the excitement of a play, speak of an unusual sense of stepping into a heightened state of awareness. In an interview conducted by author Paul Zimmerman, the Pittsburgh Steelers' Paul Martha spoke of a large change that came over him during the 1967 season. As a free safety, Martha had heard many times that he was supposed to watch the quarterback and the receiver, but doing so had always been difficult for him. As a result, he often felt outside the play, not completely in touch with what was happening. When the experience of staying in full contact with the quarterback and receiver finally clicked for Martha, he was no longer an *outsider*—"I realized I was following the quarterback all the way—and the receiver, too. It just happened. It was like I had stepped into an entirely new dimension."

Another important part of the subjective experience of peak performance is *a sense of ecstasy or joy*. Even before the run in which Roger Bannister broke the four-minute-mile barrier, he had been seduced by the empowering ecstasy of his sport. He recalled his pleasure in running through the English countryside as a youth: "I developed a basis of physical strength and an emotional, as well as physical, attraction to *the sheer joy of running*." Similarly, discus thrower Al Oerter, four-time gold medalist, reflecting on the way he felt during the Olympic Games, said, "There is no amount of money, no amount of power, no position in life that can equal that experience." Of the ecstatic moment in sport, Yuri Vlasov, world champion Russian weight lifter, said, "There is no more precious moment in life than this, *the white moment, and you will work very hard for years just to taste it again.*"

In her autobiography, Billie Jean King wrote of her moments of ecstasy in tennis: "When it happens, I want to stop the match and shout, '*That's* what it's all about.' Because it is. It's not the big prize I'm going to win at the end of the match, or anything else. It's just having done something that's totally pure and having experienced the perfect emotion."

In summary, the peak performance experience is characterized in the following way:

The athlete has an expectation of success.

The everyday world recedes, and the athlete begins to act completely "in the moment," as though an automatic pilot has been switched on.

The athlete is totally focused on the present, and concentration is so intense that actions are anticipated before they occur.

There is a sense of possessing extraordinary power, which sometimes appears to be coming from an outside source or from a new source within oneself.

There is a sense of being completely immersed in the activity, perfectly in tune with the action in which the athlete is engaged.

There is a feeling of joy and ecstasy, the "perfect emotion."

It is clear, from both Soviet research and my own work with athletes, that there are skills that can be learned that help create the peak performance frame of mind. The process of conditioning the mind in this way is really no different from the process of conditioning the body.

THE POWER OF THE PROGRAM

The foundation of every peak performer's training is contained in a single word: *program*. I would like to emblazon this word on a billboard in letters nine feet tall to emphasize this point. Without the structure provided by a clear, step-by-step training program, the athlete can waste precious hours, or even years, seeking a path to excellence down culs-du-sac where little or nothing is accomplished. In the pages ahead, I present a detailed Peak Performance Training Program, which incorporates the best of the East European methods with the best of the West.

The key to the Peak Performance Training Program is *orchestration*. Taken in isolation, each of the skills presented in the program has its own merits and limitations just as a single player on a team can only contribute to the whole but not *be* it. As everyone who has ever engaged in team sports knows, there is a certain magic that occurs when the individuals are brought together and orchestrated as a unit.

In the orchestration of peak performance skills, a powerful synthesis of human capabilities is elicited from within the individual, and it is at this point that the doors of that person's hidden reserves are flung wide open. It is important to keep the orchestration metaphor in mind as you work with this program. The individual skills presented here will be enormously enhanced as they are blended together as a whole—the *whole,* in this case, being the Peak Performance Training necessary to develop your full athletic potential.

THE PEAK PERFORMANCE TRAINING PROGRAM

SPORTS MOTIVATION ANALYSIS

Discovering the You Who Can
Become a Peak Performer

> **One of the first lessons one learns . . . is that the mind is a powerful factor in everything you do, including those exercises that seem to require a maximum of physical strength.**
>
> Joe Hyams
> *Zen in the Martial Arts*

Achieving peak performance begins with the discovery, complete acceptance, and development of skills to exercise consciously the power of *volition*. This power makes itself known in a variety of ways: as an all-encompassing desire for success, or in the feeling "I *will* do it," or simply in making the commitment to accomplish something that is particularly important to you. It embodies a certain kind of internally based motivation. Sports psychologist Linda Lewis Griffith, writing in the March 1983 issue of *Women's Sports*, stated that this kind of motivation "isn't an accidental phenomenon. It's a commitment to move toward something you want and are willing to work for."

Volition can make itself known as tenacity, single-mindedness, or stubbornness in your pursuit of a personal goal. Understanding the character of volition and exploring its potential is a vital component in your achieving peak performance.

Volition itself has no direction but is much like electrical energy, offering only a *potential* until it is "harnessed" and guided to an appropriate device. It is a potential that you activate in sports through discipline and dedication, mobilizing the powers of your body and mind. The extent to which you succeed depends on training and practice—and this means training and practice in *all* the major areas necessary for excellence in your particular sport. In the West, we have frequently developed physical training to a fine art—some say to the detriment of mental training. Although we now have evidence from the Soviet Union that under certain circumstances mental training may be far more beneficial than is physical training, mental training has only been touched upon in the United States.

In this lesson, you will establish a working relationship with your volition, an essential component of mental training.

THE WINNER'S MIND

It is a rare athlete or coach who would fail to acknowledge the importance of volition in sports. But how often do we hear talk about actually training our volition? Coaches come close when they speak of confidence. While these terms are related, the relationship has never been apparent until now. Although this is not the whole picture, confidence clearly is a *by-product* of volition. Confidence reflects the belief that we as athletes are not bound by past records, genetics, or conditioning, but that we can "operate as free beings, capable of influencing to a significant extent the course of our lives."

The portion of the above statement placed in quotes was made by researchers Elmer and Alyce Green, the American scientists mentioned earlier whose work at the Menninger Foundation came to my attention a few years before my visit to Milan. They were investigating the implications of mental training in medicine at the same time that the Soviets were researching mental training in sports. Both the Soviet and American scientists explored the possibility and subsequently proved that humans could use mental processes to exercise a level of control over their autonomic functions (as we have seen, these are the physiological processes generally believed to be outside voluntary influence and include heart rate, respiration, temperature, and blood pressure). In both the United States and the Soviet Union, learning how to exercise this control is called "self-regulation training." In describing the goals of his research project, Elmer Green said, "At the beginning of training in self-regulation we may be programmed by genetics and conditioning to a large degree, but it is the extent to which we can modify the program that is important, and it is here that we begin."

In their experiments the Greens used sophisticated electronic equipment to measure the influence of the mind on bodily functions. In the process, they evaluated yogis from India, individuals undergoing biofeedback training, and a variety of experimental systems for voluntarily altering brain-wave patterns. They found that not only were the yogis able to voluntarily alter their brain waves, heart rates, body temperatures, and other metabolic processes ordinarily considered to be regulated by the autonomic nervous system, but that the ability to voluntarily control these processes could be taught to others with little difficulty in a relatively short time.

Results of the Greens' research became important to me for a variety of reasons. One in particular was the possible relevance to my own sport, power lifting. A phenomenon occurs in power lifting that demonstrates how the exercising of volition and the resulting voluntary control of autonomic functions contribute to peak performance. The trained lifter knows that during the few seconds before a lift, total attention must be focused on the bar, and the degree to which this is done is largely determined by how much he really wants to make the lift. If his confidence is lacking or his volition not intensely focused, he simply can't make the lift; he just can't muster the necessary psychological control and muscle power. He can, however, turn away for a few moments, renew his confidence, reinforce his resolve, and rally the full force of his volition, then return to make the lift with relative ease.

The same phenomenon occurs with marathon runners when they have seemingly depleted their normal glycogen supplies at least two-thirds of the way through a race. At this point, the race can be determined by the athlete's ability to call up apparently hidden reserves, using the mind to summon additional muscle fibers to participate. Without a *strong belief* in the ability to do this, the runner simply never discovers the technique for accessing the glycogen reserves. The mechanism at work here is intriguing and deserves further exploration.

David L. Costill, director of the Human Performance Lab at Ball State University in Indiana, described this process: "In running marathon distances you learn that as you lose certain capabilities of the muscle, the only fibers that have any fuel left are fibers that require a stimulus of higher frequency—a stronger input—to fire. They have a higher threshold of recruitment. It's only when the other fibers leave you that the load is heavy enough to force the unused fibers to come into play. You concentrate to do that."

The Greens stated that "volition is the heart of the mind-body problem," and it has "unusual significance with respect to the autonomic nervous system." The Greens' premise, borne out by their research, is that each of us possesses a highly sophisticated and effective communications network between mind and body, a mechanism in which "every change in the physiological state is accompanied by an appropriate change in the mental-emotional state, conscious or unconscious, and, conversely, every change in the mental-emotional state, conscious or unconscious, is accompanied by an appropriate change in the physiological state."

Remember that confidence is a by-product of the athlete's belief in his or her volition. When that belief is particularly strong, it takes on a power all its own, a power that peak performing athletes have described as *almost palpable*. As I mentioned in the preceding chapter, it affects not only the athlete possessing it but others as well. Examples of this abound in sports history—pitcher Gene Conley, speaking of Ted Williams, once remarked, "Confidence just oozed out of him. He took something away from you even before you threw a pitch."

There is also an inner experience that frequently goes along with those moments of confidence, a sense of possessing powers that clearly transcend everyday experiences. In his biography, *My Life and the Beautiful Game,* soccer great Pele painted a particularly colorful portrait of such a moment: "I felt I could run all day without tiring, that I could dribble through any of their team or all of them, that I could almost pass through them physically."

There is considerable evidence in sports literature that there are direct correlations between self-confidence and peak performance. In a research project directed by James E. Loehr, founder of the Center for Athletic Excellence, forty-three professional and recreational athletes, representing seven different sports, were interviewed. These athletes were asked to write down their psychological experiences prior to and during a peak athletic performance. From these interviews, Loehr compiled a composite statement that characterized the athletes' perceptions of themselves: "I felt like I could do almost anything, as if I were in complete control. I really felt confident and positive."

A study of U.S. skiers training for the Olympic team revealed that even though the physical abilities of all candidates were as near equal as could be determined, those who performed best and were ultimately chosen for the team consistently expressed positive attitudes about their abilities. Those who did not make the team were typically negative or tentative about their performance abilities. Drawing from this and other examples, psychologists Norman E. Weitzberg and Kerry Paul Altman, in a paper presented at the 1978 Convention of the California State Psychological Association, stated: "Attitudes and expectations are significant determinants of performance." In reviewing a broad cross section of studies, the same researchers found that "a positive attitude and high expectations for achievement are widely acknowledged."

Thomas Tutko, cofounder of the Institute of Athletic Motivation, professor of psychology at San Jose State University, and one of the most widely respected authorities on sports psychology, goes one step further. He suggests direct links between attitude and muscle: "Your emotions affect every cell in your body. Mind and body, mental and physical, are intertwined."

While Tutko's statement provides us with an important clue about the peak performance experience, champion surfer Midget Farrelly provides us with a practical, action-oriented viewpoint in his book *The Surfing Life:* "Sometimes you reach a point of being so coordinated, so completely balanced, that you feel you can be anything—anything at all. At times like this I find I can run up to the front of the board and stand on the nose when pushing through a broken wave; I can goof around, put myself in an impossible position, and then pull out of it. . . . An extra bit of confidence like that can carry you through, and you can do things that are just about impossible."

MAKING IT HAPPEN FOR YOU

For most athletes, the peak performance is only a coincidence, a serendipitous moment when everything comes together in just the right combination. It is difficult to take much credit for achievements until we perceive and assume control of the power our own beliefs, actions, and experiences play in our successes. All too often we consciously or subconsciously choose not to see the relationship between volition and personal achievement. The moment passes too quickly, with, at best, an illusion that we were briefly the fortunate possessors of transient powers that we could never hope to rally voluntarily. How often we fail to let ourselves see that we have the freedom to be successful—and if only we would exercise that freedom!

Abraham Maslow saw that there were people in all walks of life who knew, either intuitively or through rigorous discipline, how to harness their volition and thus to approach, equal, or improve upon their peak performances time and time again.

These were what Maslow called "self-actualizing" people, those who assumed control of the mental and physical skills to perform optimally on a fairly consistent basis. Maslow wrote: "Self-actualizing people, those who have come to a high level of maturation, health, and self-fulfillment, have so much to teach us that sometimes they seem almost like a different breed of human beings."

My experience in Milan made it quite clear that basic skills for achieving self-actualization, at least in sports, could be learned, and that there are basic skills common to superathletes that could be systematized, as the Soviets had done. In working with other people and applying some of the techniques I myself had experienced, I had to agree with a statement made by Elmer Green about the promise of volition: "As we begin to realize that we are not totally the victims of our genetics, conditioning, and accidents, changes begin to happen in our lives, nature begins to respond to us in a new way, and the things that we visualize, even though unlikely, begin to happen with increasing frequency. Our bodies *tend to do what they are told to do, if we know how to tell them.*"

Learning how to tell our bodies is the trick, of course. Control of the autonomic functions, whether for greater well-being or to increase performance levels in sports, is a subtle process, an act of integrating rather than one of imposing our will or physical strength over our natural capacities. As the Greens have stated, "It is important to realize that it [voluntary control of the autonomic functions] is not accomplished by force. . . . It is done by imagining and visualizing the intended change while in a relaxed state."

SUCCESS IS NOT ACCIDENTAL

Peak performers distinguish themselves from those who merely do well first and foremost by assuming *active responsibility for their successes.* As a peak performer, you will know that your triumphs come about not because luck favors you but because of the active responsibility you have taken. Your awareness of your actions and how they contribute to your success is an essential part of becoming a peak performer.

Being able to perceive that the products of your volition—everything you think, feel, and do—ultimately contribute to the outcome of your efforts requires a new kind of responsibility that, for many people, may seem to oppose everything they've been taught. Therefore, your first assignment is to focus completely on self, assuming responsibility and accountability for what you do. Make conscious efforts to see and acknowledge what it is you do that is, indeed, significant and thus refutes all notions that your successes are pure luck. The exercises at the end of this lesson will help you to understand the power of your own volition and will also help you to see that the stronger and more constant your belief in volition, the more positive and consistent your efforts to suceed will be.

Psychiatrist Roberto Assagioli stated that of all our inner powers, volition should be given priority. Its training and use, he wrote in his book *Psychosynthesis,* "constitute the foundation of all endeavors." He provided two reasons for this. The first is that volition (or "the will," as he termed it) is at the core of our being. It is, in effect, the nucleus of the self, without which that self would cease to be. The second is that volition is the part of us that comes fully into play in "deciding what is to be done, in applying all the necessary means for its realization, and in persisting in the task in the face of all obstacles and difficulties."

In *Beyond Biofeedback,* the Greens voiced their belief that volition is "the key problem of our day, because control of the individual by society and by the state has taken away some of our own responsibility for our health, our education, and our activities." In this respect it is ironic that the Soviets, whose governmental policies are frequently attacked for oppressing individual freedoms, should have become the world leaders in the mental training of athletes.

At the International Society for Sport Psychology's Fifth World Sport Psychology Congress, held in Ottawa, Canada, in 1981, Polish sports psychologist Tadeusz Rychta reflected on what he called the new psychology of training. Rychta described the new training programs as "one of those forms of human activity that favors self-perfection and self-actualization" and that encourages "all-around human personality development." He added that "sport training, through its physical actions, activates those human sources which develop an athlete's personality, improving physical and psychological skills and [helping the individual to] discover unlimited possibilities of human mind and body."

We thus begin our mental training program with exercises that immediately focus on volition, *the foundation of all human endeavors*. In these first exercises, you will identify the you who can become a peak performer through a process that allows you to discover more of the power of your own volition and the nature of the experiences that strengthen it. From this material you will be able to develop a training program that makes for more use of your volition. This material is a prerequisite to the lesson on goal-setting and strategy that follows.

IDENTIFYING YOUR VOLITION   Phase One

Time: Three 30-minute sessions

Benefits: Through this exercise, you locate in yourself the personal power we call volition or will power and you identify the individualized kinds of experiences that fuel this important mental resource for you.

We all have many sides to our personalities, many selves within, each defined by the various roles we assume in daily life—as spouse, lover, parent, sibling, in work and play, and as athletes. Each of us is alternately capable of being heroic or cowardly, wise or foolish, weak or strong, insightful or obtuse. However, the you who can become a peak performer is unique. This is the self that emerges in the face of a challenge, be it in your vocation, in recreation, in your personal relationships, or in your sport. It is the self that seeks new experiences, that enjoys the thoughts and feelings that accompany your accomplishments in those fields of interest that are closest to you. It is the self that is motivated by the change brought about through your own efforts.

Few people know this aspect of themselves so well that they can summon it at will. Yet, being in touch with this self is essential in Peak Performance Training. What you will learn by doing this exercise is that your volition is fueled by many sources—from past experiences of your own successes to recollections of live sporting events, books, and movies.

Since Peak Performance Training is directed to this self which exercises powerful volition, we need to become familiar with it, to know it, get inside it, be able to rely on it, use it, and even *become* it, at will. How do we come to know this self? We do so in the same way biographers would get to know their subjects. Biographers attempt to record as many details as possible in order to tell the reader what the subjects of the biographies did to realize their accomplishments. What did they think about, and what were their opinions? With what kinds of choices were they faced in their lives? How did they make the decisions they eventually made? What kinds of memories and what feelings spurred them on through the more challenging or difficult times? Were there special skills they applied that were important in doing what they did?

In the Peak Performance Training Program, the technique used for drawing together this information about you, for creating a clear image of the self who can become a peak performer, is called "clustering." This technique, for which we will, in a few pages, be providing clear how-to instructions, was developed by Gabrielle Lusser Rico as part of an innovative writing program. In her book, *Writing the Natural Way,* Rico calls this technique a "nonlinear brainstorming process akin to free association." She explains further that through clustering, "we naturally come up with a multitude of choices from a part of our mind where the experiences of a lifetime mill and mingle." This process is useful for training peak performers for the same reasons that it is useful in writing—it provides access to the "experiences of a lifetime." For our purposes here, these are the experiences that have contributed to important personal achievements.

This exercise reveals the powerful role that volition plays in your life, at times guiding your choices in such things as how you will spend your time during the day—pushing you, for example, to make time for your sport, even when you have an extremely busy schedule—and at times seeming to act like a magnet or other invisible force, pulling you toward experiences that, in ways not immediately obvious, help you to realize your goals fully.

Figure 1–1 is an example of clustering, showing the satellite clusters emanating from a central point, and detailing what the person who created this chart felt were important elements of a personal achievement that he called "Running the Dipsea Trail." Notice the variety of material contained in the satellite clusters, from the simple exclamation "Joy!!" to the piece of personal philosophy that "without accessing the strongest parts of myself I could not run this race," to the obscure note about a scene from a book describing a runner.

This is a free-form method of notation, so don't be afraid to experiment, invent, and allow your mind to wander. Allow one notation or memory to trigger another, as they naturally will. Remember, this is a *nonlinear brainstorming* process, and *should not be orderly or immediately make sense* to you. Let your mind wander, guided only by the most rudimentary suggestions from memory.

Relax as you make your notes. Send your *inner censor* on vacation (this censor is the critical part of you that might suggest that something you are thinking or feeling is unimportant or irrelevant). Let your mind play with the various elements you bring into the picture. You may find that as you note one thing, several others will come to mind. For example, in Figure 1–1, the athlete's statement "I discover me" suggests several other thoughts—"uniqueness," "my own motion," and "whistle my own tune." (This is an indication that the exercise is really working.) Note all of these, even when they seem only indirectly related.

Figure 1–1 Running the Dipsea Trail. Tom P., the runner who did the cluster above, makes numerous notes that refer to very solitary experiences. The abundance of notes such as "I discover me," "responsibility to myself," and "whistle my own tune," and the absence of notes describing his associations with other people (fellow runners, coaches, family members, or spectators) indicates that the most powerful elements of his running experience are in the realm of what he, upon examining his cluster, called "self-discovery."

Preparation

Have ready a pencil and a few sheets of blank 8½ × 11 paper. Do the exercise when you will have no interruptions for at least thirty minutes.

Instructions

Step One

Recall a moment when you performed extremely well in competition or perhaps achieved a very important personal goal,

Recall, event making it feel important

or even simply a moment when you experienced great happiness or exhilaration in something you did. This need not be an athletic event. It might be something relevant to business, education, a hobby, or a personal relationship, such as resolving a conflict with another person or making a personal contact that was important to you. What you'll be working with here will not have anything to do with how important your peak experience was to the rest of the world but only with how it affected you. The ideal choice is an event or achievement you recall as being among the most exciting, the most satisfying, and requiring the greatest investment of effort on your part. Choose three such events.

Begin now by jotting down a brief description of one of the experiences. Draw a heavy line around it. Be certain to leave ample room in the surrounding space, since you will be making other notes there.

Step Two

Sit in a comfortable chair, close your eyes, and relive this experience. Recall as many details as possible to make the memory real to you—where you were, the people you were with, and the weather. How did you feel? Call up, if you can, the thoughts and feelings that went through your mind at the time or note the ones that come to mind now as you try to recall this experience. Were you proud? Relieved? Ecstatic? Exhilarated? Were you awed? Did you have a sense of your own capabilities, your own power? Write in a few words a description of what you felt and thought, and draw a circle around each word or group of words.

Step Three

Ask yourself what things in your life are associated with your peak experience. Consider books you have read, what you have learned from friendships, movies you've seen, sporting events—anything significant that contributed to the peak experience. Jot these down, circle them, and join them with the growing cluster. Try connecting the various elements of your cluster with arrows, straight lines, and so on, choosing whatever forms express the things you want them to express. For example, a solid line might represent a strong link between two elements, while a dotted line might represent a weak link or association. Similarly, a line with an arrow might represent a strong association or direction but not a direct link with another element.

Step Four

Now focus on what things you did directly and deliberately to accomplish the event. For example, if your peak experience was in sports, what was your training regimen? Make notes on your choices of equipment or training partners. If the experience involved something such as landing a job you wanted, did your formal education or prior employment record help you qualify? Note *any* outstanding details about your education or your employment history that were instrumental.

Step Five

Repeat steps two through four to complete clusters for the other two peak experiences you have chosen.

Discussion

Notice as you look over the sample clusters, (Figures 1–1, 1–2, and 1–3), as well as the ones you have made, that a great variety of experience is usually associated with any important accomplishment. Since the nature and character of volition varies with each individual, we cannot always predict what will be valuable or important. The clustering exercises offer a consistent means for examining and evaluating this unique human quality. Athletes in particular will find that volition is strengthened by a lifetime of experience, often drawing as much from childhood recollections and nonsports activities as from more immediate experiences such as winning an important athletic competition. Don't be surprised if while working on a cluster you find yourself making notes that appear irrelevant or only remotely connected to the accomplishment you are exploring. Jot them down, *regardless* of how unrelated they may seem to be at the time.

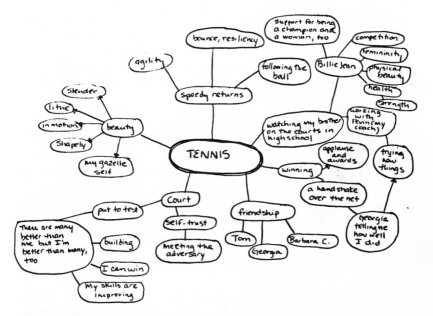

Figure 1–2 Tennis. Patricia T., the tennis player who did this cluster, displays a broad variety of volitional concerns. She is interested in the social contacts provided by the game and in putting herself to the test of competition ("There are many better than me but I'm better than many, too"), she finds in the game an identification with a champion (Billie Jean King), and she enjoys the benefits of physical health and beauty that playing the game provides.

When completed, your cluster will serve as an individualized record of the events that have fueled your volition and increased your belief in yourself or strengthened your confidence. Looking back through this method at the experiences that you drew upon or that reinforced your volitional power, you discover important things about the peak performer within *you!*

Everything associated with an important personal achievement reflects on the individualized needs of the heart and mind of the self within you that can become a peak performer. For example, while training with others may be important for some athletes, it may be distracting and unproductive for you. It is important to recognize that what excites one person may be

Figure 1–3 Swimming Four Miles the First Time. The first thing we notice in the above cluster, by Fred B., is in the title he gives to the cluster: "Swimming Four Miles the First Time." The title immediately suggests the fulfillment of a goal toward which he had worked for an extended period. This is borne out by some of the satellite clusters: "Two years of hard work rewarded!" "surprised by my own ability," and "Education is change." Upon reflection of these notations, Fred said that he has always set goals for himself, and that he enjoys "putting myself to a test and measuring the progress by my improvements, similar to plotting out a trip on a map." He also makes notations such as "Going under the sprinkler on a hot day in New York" and "the water dance," which suggest that he derives aesthetic and sensual pleasures from swimming. Fred commented that he had never realized how much setting goals for himself actually excited and motivated him, and that he would, in the future, pay much closer attention to his use of this technique.

dull or just not important to another, even though both people are involved in training at the same level for the same sport. By recognizing these differences and knowing your own individual needs, you can become adept at identifying the experiences that spur you on and exert a positive force on your volition; you can thus learn to meet your own needs in this, rather than blindly following another person's prescription. This individualization of the training program has been named by most peak performers as a key ingredient to success.

EVALUATING YOUR VOLITION   Phase Two

Time: One 15-minute session

Benefits: This exercise provides an instrument for characterizing the kinds of experiences that have maximum volitional impact for you, so that you can select the most effective training experiences in the future.

In this, the second phase of the lesson, you will use a checklist to evaluate the clusters you have previously completed in order to make some general observations about the kinds of experiences that fuel your volition. For example, you may discover that most high-volition experiences you recorded in the clusters were in activities that you did alone. In Figure 1–1, you saw this *solo* theme of the runner's experiences noted again and again: "Running alone on the beach," "I discover me," "my own motion," and "In competition the other runners are no more or less a challenge than the hills or distance I run." In evaluating his volition cluster using the following list, this person gave a high rating to number six ("Feelings of well-being") and number eight ("Solo workouts"), both of which focus on the runner's relationship to himself rather than to other runners or to the response of spectators or coaches to his performance. By contrast, the tennis player in Figure 1–2 found that "friendship," "competition," and "applause and awards" were volitionally important to her.

The purpose of this exercise is not to test your responses, but instead to allow you to discover the kinds of experiences that are particularly important or exciting to you and that may thus strengthen your volition. By having this information at your disposal, you can plan training activities for their highest volitional impact. For example, if you discover, like the runner above, that solo training appeals to you more than does running with other people, you would know that you can make the most progress by seeking out solo training experiences, knowing they would provide you with maximum volitional power.

How you rate your experiences—high, medium, or low—is purely subjective. To establish a criterion for this, simply scan your clusters until you identify one experience in which you felt excited, optimistic, and positive about your performance. This experience is considered to be of high volitional impact, and the feelings you have here become the measure for evaluating high ratings of other experiences. Experiences that you've written down but that seem only mildly important to you are of low volitional impact and should be noted as such.

Go through the following list point by point, searching for manifestations of each point in your clusters. Obviously, not everyone will find examples of every point in their clusters; the purpose here is to discover what *does* apply and to use that knowledge to your advantage in putting together your training program. Also, you may want to rate yourself on some of the points even though they are not represented in your clusters.

Preparation
Have the clusters you have completed available. Do this exercise when you will not be disturbed for at least fifteen minutes.

Instructions
Using your clusters as your references, rate the statements according to their volitional impact on you. Circle "L" for low volitional impact, "M" for medium volitional impact, and "H" for high volitional impact.

1. *Action:* Taking an active part in training and/or in competition.

    L   M   H

2. *Spectator:* Watching other athletes either in training or in competition.

    L   M   H

3. *Coaching:* Learning techniques and strategies from lectures and talks, books, films, and so on.

    L   (M)   (H)

4. *Past experiences:* Thinking about or reliving past experiences in your sport—winning competitions, experiencing major accomplishments—or just recalling enjoyable moments.

    L   M   (H)

5. *Contemplating the future:* Thinking about or constructing mental images of future goals or experiences in sport.

    L   (M)   (H)

6. *Feelings of well-being:* Mental or physical feelings or sensations associated with being in shape or being able to perform well.

    L   (M)   H

7. *Competition:* Being challenged by the prospect of breaking a record (either a personal best or a public record).

    (L)   M   (H)

8. *Solo workouts:* Working out alone, perhaps competing with a personal record, rather than competing with other people or seeking out their companionship as an integral part of the workout.

    (L)   M   (H)

9. *Companionship:* Working out with others either for their companionship and support or for the stimulus of competition.

    (L——M)   (H)

10. *Feedback:* Discussions with coaches, other athletes, and friends to receive constructive criticism of your performance and/or progress.

    (L)   M   (H)

11. *External motivators:* Meeting or exceeding standards or expectations of friends, coaches, relatives, and so on.

    L   M   (H)

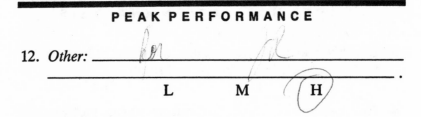

12. *Other:* _____

_____ .
              L   M   H

Examples of Volition Evaluations
Tom P. (Figure 1–1) made the following evaluation of his volition:

1. *Action*   H
2. *Spectator*   L
3. *Coaching*   L
4. *Past experiences*   L
5. *Contemplating the future*   M
6. *Feelings of well-being*   H
7. *Competition*   M
8. *Solo workouts*   H
9. *Companionship*   L
10. *Feedback*   L
11. *External motivators*   L
12. *Other:* I have a very private sense of how I want to feel about myself, something I'm always aware of, though I don't think I've ever put it into words.   H

Patricia T. (Figure 1–2) evaluated her volition as follows:

1. *Action*   H
2. *Spectator*   M
3. *Coaching*   M
4. *Past experiences*   M
5. *Contemplating the future*   M
6. *Feelings of well-being*   H
7. *Competition*   H
8. *Solo workouts*   · L

9. *Companionship*   H
10. *Feedback*   H
11. *External motivators*   H
12. *Other:* Lately I've become intrigued by the ways I am affected by the pressure of competition. I used to associate all competition with either me or the other person losing. I'm beginning to think it's the only way to do one's best. Want to study more about what other athletes think about this.   H

Fred B. (Figure 1–3) evaluated his volition as follows:

1. *Action*   H
2. *Spectator*   M
3. *Coaching*   M
4. *Past experiences*   H
5. *Contemplating the future*   H
6. *Feelings of well-being*   H
7. *Competition*   H
8. *Solo workouts*   M
9. *Companionship*   M
10. *Feedback*   L
11. *External motivators*   H
12. *Other:* I find that setting goals and succeeding at achieving those goals is a challenge that excites me on a volitional level almost as much as the activity of swimming itself.   H

Discussion
Bear in mind that your answers to these questions represent individualized needs or preferences, dictated by the personality of the *you* who can become a peak performer. These are the kinds of experiences that have acted as positive forces on you in the past, and using what you have learned as a guideline,

you can develop a plan for the future, choosing training experiences that you know have been helpful to you. Phase Three, The Goal Profile, shows you how to do this in a systematic way.

THE GOAL PROFILE   Phase Three

Time: One 30-minute session

Benefits: Here you create clusters to provide a picture of the training experiences that will have the greatest effect on you in terms of your volition.

In Phase One of this lesson, the technique of clustering was used to revive pictures of past accomplishments and the experiences associated with them. Clustering is also used here in developing a plan for future accomplishments and for the experiences that can contribute to their realization. You'll use the information you have discovered through the first two phases of this lesson to begin developing a training plan to make your present goal a reality.

Preparation

Have paper and pencil ready. Have the clusters and evaluations you've completed available for easy reference. Do the exercise at a time when you will not be disturbed for at least thirty minutes.

Instructions

Choose a goal—something you want to accomplish in the near future. It may be modest or ambitious, but in any case it should express a strong feeling about something you want to accomplish very much. As in Phase One, this can be anything from learning to run two miles per day smoothly and effortlessly to winning a game, tournament, or a special award.

Write a brief description of your goal in the center of a blank sheet of paper. Circle it with a heavy line, as you did in Phase One. You can now begin clustering.

Refer to Phase Two, and note the statements characterizing the experiences that have high volitional impact for you. For example, let's say that you have found competition and solo workouts important in the past, definitely strengthening your confidence that you have the self-determination and free choice to achieve your goals.

Now think about all the ways you can experience both competition and solo workouts. Relax as you do this, letting your mind run free. Make clusters of each idea or feeling that excites you about your future goal (see Figures 1–4, 1–5, and 1–6, which show clusters for competition, solo workouts, and goal-setting).

Continue going through your list of statements from Phase Two, recording clusters of experiences you feel can help you realize your present goal.

Review all twelve points in Phase Two thoroughly. Work slowly, trusting the process of automatic association that normally arises as you focus on any subject relevent to training that might appear in this list.

Discussion

Upon finishing this phase of the lesson you will have a profile that suggests what experiences you should seek out to foster and reinforce your volitional power. Some things you record here will have direct benefits for physical training as well as for mental training, but keep in mind that mental training is your priority here. Occasionally, athletes fail to record the physical training exercises that they know are important to the total picture but that do not excite them volitionally. If you are unable to clarify where you should record physical training, rest assured that you need not record it in this exercise at all; you will have the opportunity to do this in Lesson 2 the goal-setting and strategy chapter.

Figure 1–4 Running the Bay to Breakers Race. Tom P., whose cluster on Running the Dipsea Trail we have examined in Figure 1–1, did the above goal profile. Here we see plans for more solitary training experiences, which he previously found to have a high volitional impact for him. As a training plan for running the demanding San Francisco Bay to Breakers race, Tom identifies specific activities that had high volitional impact for him and that will help him attain his training goal—everything from concentrating on the motions of his own body to rereading a scene from a novel that had impressed him, so that he could hold that image in his mind when he ran.

SUMMARY

All athletic accomplishments begin with *volition*; that is, the desire and willpower necessary to suceed. Volition affects more than thoughts and feelings—it affects physical performance. Experience, as well as scientific evidence, shows that strength, responsiveness, stamina, precision of movement, balance, and coordination are all influenced by volition.

Figure 1–5 Improving My Tennis. Patricia T., whose first cluster appeared as Figure 1–2, decided to focus her attention on three areas: feelings of well-being, competition, and spectator time, all of which she had recorded in evaluating her volition. All three of these categories, she felt, rated very high on her volitional scale and would contribute to her improving her tennis game.

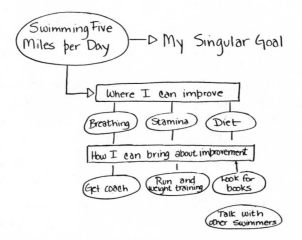

Figure 1–6 Swimming Five Miles Per Day. Recognizing the extent to which goal-setting was a strong volitional factor for him, Fred B. (from Figure 1–3) made up a goal profile that focused his attention entirely on this aspect of his volitional response. His profile offers a particularly good example of the variety of forms these clusters may take.

Just as we can train physically for maximum performance in a sport, so it is now possible to train for it mentally as well. Volition is at the core of this training. For the individual athlete, volition is strengthened by some training experiences and weakened by others. These are determined by the individual's particular needs, tastes, and personality. In order to maximize the volitional power, and in the process maximize physical performance, we need to thoroughly familiarize ourselves with the individual needs and responses of the *self within us* who can become a peak performer. We need to discover what kinds of experiences have fueled volition in the past, and what kinds of experiences we should seek in order to do the same, or better, in the future.

Phase One of this lesson revealed how to identify your volition by using clustering to explore the kinds of training experiences that have strengthened your volition in the past.

Phase Two helped you evaluate your volition and thus generalize about the experiences of high volitional impact. This skill allows you to recall general experiences that elevated volition in past training in order to do the same in future training programs.

Phase Three showed how to prepare a goal profile developed from high-impact training experiences for succeeding in future athletic goals.

The next step, after identifying volition and the ways we can maximize its influence on physical performance, is to design a plan of action for fully channeling this power toward achieving specific athletic goals. That's what you will be doing in Lesson 2.

APPLICATIONS FOR THIS LESSON OUTSIDE SPORTS

Career/Business: As in sports, peak performance in the business world begins by identifying and focusing one's energies on activities of high volitional impact. Having interviewed many peak performers in the business world over the years, it is very clear to me that all have a deep personal interest in the activities they are doing on a daily basis, an interest that is more powerful than material reward or merely getting the job done. Their drive comes from *within,* from being in touch with the interests and experiences in their career or business that provide high volitional impact.

In the same way that you used clustering to identify the kinds of things that fuel your volition in sport, you can identify the kinds of things that fuel your volition in your career. For example, one of the partners of a computer company in California's Silicon Valley used clustering to assess his work on sales campaigns. Although he had been taking responsibility for the total program—from conceptualization through the daily supervision of the sales staff—much of what he did frustrated him, and he was certain his best talents were not being utilized in ways that might benefit the company.

In the process of doing a number of clusters, this executive discovered that his main interests, and his greatest talents, lay in the conceptualization of campaigns. The rest of his duties were actually robbing him of time he might be spending in that conceptualization process. As a result of this discovery, he reorganized his department, delegating the responsibility of the supervision of the sales staff to someone else and leaving himself more time for conceptualization. Following this reorganization, this man put together the most successfui sales campaign of his company's history.

Clustering is also an invaluable tool for brainstorming. Begin with the subject for a memo, an idea for a new product, or an organizational problem as the center of the cluster. Then use the same free-association process I've described in his lesson to record the elements of the problem on which you are working. You will be surprised how automatically this process unfolds, ultimately providing you with a graphic presentation of the problem.

At one of my workshops, a woman who owned a large travel agency used the clustering technique to brainstorm a set of three European travel packages. She put the title of the tour at the center of the cluster, then drew up satellites around it of all the elements that came to her mind that would make such a package attractive. When the cluster was finished she went back and made careful choices on the basis of scheduling, availability, and price. The end product of her efforts was a set of carefully thought out travel packages that appealed to a diverse cross section of potential buyers, from *budget* to *luxury class* travelers.

Personal: In your personal life use clustering for brainstorming personal decisions—anything from sorting out what is disturbing you in a conflict with a close friend or your mate to education and career planning. For example, a young woman does a cluster to identify the source of her annoyance with her fiancé. She focuses on two issues that disturb her—his tardiness when they make arrangements to meet in public places and his failure to consult her when making decisions that affect her. With the clearer focus she has gained, she presents him with these problems as well as with some suggestions for alternative actions he might consider.

Another example: a man in his thirties feels bored with the way he is spending his free time. He does a cluster to evaluate his leisure activities and discovers that they fail to connect with anything with a high volitional rating for him. He does another cluster around possible alternatives, including a number that he has never considered before. On the basis of his discoveries he decides to go back to school for additional education that may change virtually every aspect of his life. He also remembers a "forgotten" college interest in public service activities that leads him to many new friendships.

As in sports, discovering and identifying areas of high volitional impact lead to change, either in the short-term or in long-range plans. The goal-setting techniques described in Lesson 2 provide an orderly framework for bringing about the required changes.

Lesson 2

UNVEILING YOUR MISSION

Goal-setting Techniques for Fully

Actualizing Your Athletic Ambitions

Man has his future within him,
dynamically alive at this present
moment.
—Abraham Maslow
psychologist

In Lesson 2 you will discover more about volition and how to assume greater control of its power. By developing what peak performers call a *sense of mission,* a passionate belief in a personal philosophy that establishes the basis for setting goals, you can control your own energies and generate that special drive essential for excelling in your sport. You will learn techniques widely used in identifying and establishing goals. You will also learn how to prepare a blueprint for successful goal achievement based on the principle of "divide and conquer." The ultimate goal is reduced to a series of smaller goals, each having a high probability of achievement. This process builds self-confidence and allows visible, positive progress to further motivate and inspire the you who can become a peak performer.

GOAL-SETTING AND MENTAL IMAGERY

Without a doubt, the most dramatic contribution to the advancement of goal-setting skills in recent years has been the Soviets' introduction of visualization. Use of this skill substantially increased the effectiveness of goal-setting, which up to then had been little more than a dull listing procedure. As used in goal-setting, visualization is a refinement of mental rehearsal techniques developed by the Russians. During mental rehearsal, athletes create mental images of the exact movements they want to emulate in their sport. The Soviets found that mental images act as precursors in the process of generating neuromuscular impulses, which regulate and control physical movement. These images are holographic (three dimensional) and function primarily at the subliminal level. The holographic imaging mechanism enables you to quickly solve spatial problems such as assembling a complex machine, choreographing a dance routine, or running visual images of plays through your mind. The mental images act as three-dimensional blueprints for encoding the information required to effect exact sequences and ranges of physical movement in athletic activity. In the process of goal-setting, we create detailed mental images of actions and desired outcomes—a phenomenon that is still being studied. According to researchers, we enhance and accelerate our physical learning process by combining mental imagery and physical training.

The roots of Soviet use of self-regulation training can be traced to the work of Ivan Pavlov, who conducted pioneering research with the *conditioned reflex response*. Although he did not deal directly with mental imagery, Pavlov did provide the scientific rationale for self-regulation training that would ultimately incorporate visualization techniques. He proved that certain responses could be elicited by an external stimulus. His now classic experiments demonstrated that by hearing a bell rung at feeding time, laboratory dogs became conditioned to associate a ringing bell with feeding. He also showed that once the dogs were conditioned, they would salivate when the bell was rung even when no food was present. It is a long way from

Pavlov's experiments to modern self-regulation training in sports, but the association is acknowledged by virtually every Soviet sports psychologist.

In later experiments, Bulgarian psychiatrist Georgi Lozanov and others demonstrated that "suggestions" in the form of words and phrases (such as we might use in goal-setting) could initiate conditioned responses in humans. Lozanov adapted Pavlov's theories for use in human experiments. Also, when Lozanov applied his own theory of "suggestology," his subjects learned to alter certain physiological functions, improved their mental and physical health, and enhanced learning skills such as those involving high-speed numerical calculations and rapid learning of new languages. Lozanov substantiated what Pavlov had professed years earlier, that "suggestion is the most simplified and the most typical conditioned reflex in man."

While Pavlov pointed the way and Lozanov added to his work, it was Alexander Romen, also a Russian, who refined techniques for shaping exact behavior through words and mental imagery. Because Romen included both *physical* and *mental* response conditioning, his experiments in self-regulation training surpassed anything Pavlov or Lozanov had done. Electromyograms, a method for measuring the electrical impulses that occur in muscles just prior to actual movement, revealed that muscles actually perform the physical activity imagined or suggested by words. Romen showed that psychoneurological factors that produce specific muscular responses in humans can be "programmed" in advance of the performance of that activity through mental imagery. Thus, mental imagery becomes an invaluable tool in achieving peak performance in sports.

Goal-setting is the first step in effectively using mental imagery and language to produce highly complex courses of action that will lead to the achievement of peak performance. It combines language and mental imagery to produce what is essentially a mental road map, or blueprint, for the more in-depth mental training that will follow.

Although goal-setting is not new to Western athletes, it takes on new meaning when considered in the context of the mental training techniques developed by the Soviets and the

East Germans. Finely detailed goal-setting provides not only a plan of action but also strong guidelines for creating the appropriate mental images and phrases that will have an optimal effect on performance. The importance of precision and depth cannot be overstated. In my experiences in Milan, this fact became evident not only in my talks with the Soviets but in their demonstrations at the gym as well. Romen, too, has been particularly adamant about this point, stating that "close attention must be given to the construction of formulas. Phraseology should be handled with the same care with which a surgeon wields his scalpel." The importance of such close attention to accuracy and detail must not be underemphasized, for without it your efforts will not be effective. For this reason, all the athletes I work with are required to execute the goal-setting process, the blueprint for athletic excellence, with a very fine eye for detail and precision.

BEYOND GOAL-SETTING

Through my interviews with peak performers, I have become particularly fascinated with the fact that these athletes possess a common characteristic that is closely allied with goal-setting but that, in a peculiar way, also stands alone and deserves attention: with few exceptions, peak performers are highly motivated by a deep and personal sense of *mission,* which is distinctly different from the highly specific and measurable goals each person may set. I am reminded of the words of Yuri Vlasov, the Russian weight lifter who, when asked about his mission in sports, spoke of the intense personal delight he experienced during the peak of what he called a "victorious effort": "There is no more precious moment in life than this . . . and you will work very hard for years just to taste it again." (Surprisingly, however, learning how to get in touch with one's sense of mission is apparently not included in Soviet athletic training.) Along with this strong sense of mission, all peak performers possess an attitude of keen intentionality and delight, as opposed to the all-too-frequent determination-relief cycle of everyday life—that is, determination to get the work completed, and relief when it is done.

Material on getting in touch with your sense of mission appears as the first exercise in this lesson. The plan is as follows. You will begin by making a mission statement. You will be guided toward your own sense of mission through a series of questions that I have found to be extremely helpful for both groups and individuals. Following these questions, you will find step-by-step instructions for establishing a long-term goal that will enable you to ultimately achieve your own mission. You will then learn how to plan the steps that will carry you toward your mission through the achievement of a series of short-term goals, each ensuring a high probability of success. The final phase of this lesson will show you how to create mental images based on your mission and goal-setting exercises; these will become blueprints for the actions that will enable you to become a peak performer.

MISSION STATEMENT   Phase One

Time: One 30-minute session

Benefits: You discover the personal philosophy and purpose that motivates you in your sport.

The mission statement is a summation of your personal philosophy. What are your *private reasons* for wanting to accomplish a special goal in your sport? This personal, *subjective* statement should be distinguished from the goal itself, which is an *objective* statement about a specific athletic achievement and can be quantitatively measured. For example, you might train to run a marathon and have as your mission statement "I want that incredible feeling of really being in command of myself that I get from pushing my body to the outer limits." The goal statement of the same mission might be "To run 26 miles and finish in the top 100."

It is not always easy to get in touch with your personal philosophy about sports. In every group of athletes I work with, I always find a few who say, "I do it because I like it." I ask these people to look deeper. What is it *exactly* that they like about the athletic experience? Does it have anything to do with how they feel about their bodies? Is there something about competing with others and learning how they measure up that excites them? Is there something they want to explore about pushing themselves to their limits? Is there a greater mission, such as the one sometimes expressed by world-class athletes, of setting out to break records in order to once again redefine the athletic limits of the human race? This exercise will help you to look deeply inside yourself and explore your reasons for being involved in your particular sport. Your answers can become the primary motivational force for all you do in your sport and will allow you to concentrate both physical and mental energy on peak performance of that activity.

While I was employed as a mathematician and computer analyst on the Apollo moon shot, I experienced as never before or since the magnitude of what can be achieved through the power of people sharing a mission. There was a goal, to be sure, which was to build a space vehicle, the LEM module, of certain dimensions and capabilities. But this was not the source of power for the people working on the project. What sparked everyone's imagination and harnessed powers few had known they possessed was the realization that they were taking part in a project that would fulfill one of mankind's oldest dreams; they had a *mission*. I saw men and women of average capabilities tapping resources of personal energy and creativity that resulted in extraordinary human accomplishments. I saw their excitement and pride come alive, affecting everyone around them, kindling imaginations with the possibilities that arose from what we were trying to accomplish. One thing became very clear to me—it is not the goal, but the ultimate *mission* that kindles the imagination, motivating us toward ever higher levels of human achievement.

Do we all have a mission in sports? In workshops all over the country, attended by businesspeople, students, athletes, housewives, other people from all walks of life, I have found it to be relatively rare to encounter people who do not have a mission in their sport. Each of us, it seems, has a deep personal reason for doing what we do in our sport. What's more, the reasoning or philosophy behind our intent is seldom very difficult to discover.

Preparation

Have paper and pencil ready. Allow for at least thirty minutes of uninterrupted time.

Instructions

Explore the following leads, as you think about making a mission statement, to get in touch with your own reasons. Write down your thoughts, either as a list or in a cluster (using the clustering techniques you learned in Lesson 1).

What *feelings* do you experience when you are enjoying your sport the most? Are they feelings of victory? Peacefulness? Satisfaction that you are doing something extremely well? A feeling of having perfect control? A sense of being in touch with your physical strength, of *mind-body* integration?

Have people influenced you in your sport? For example, do you have any athletic heroes or heroines? Think about what these people and their accomplishments mean to you. How did they change your personal history? What things do you most admire about these people? For example, did they overcome great obstacles to achieve very high levels of performance? Is it that they are able to make full use of their human capabilities? Is it that they express a degree of self-confidence or faith in themselves that you find admirable? Try to get in touch with your own thoughts and feelings about athletes that you think about or admire.

Is there someone in your life, such as a friend, parent, training partner, or coach, who has influenced your interest in sports? If so, what is it about your relationship with this person that motivates you toward accomplishing whatever it is you wish to do in your sport? Write down your thoughts and give yourself time to think about them.

Do you have a personal philosophy that is expressed in other than athletic endeavors that you feel can also be expressed athletically?

All these questions lead you to discovery of the roots of your *personal mission* in sports. This is the stuff, the essence, of your volition, from which your mission statement is made. When considering each of these questions, think them over carefully and slowly. Spend some time with the thoughts and feelings that arise for you. Then, consolidate them into a single, clear statement. The final result is your mission statement.

Examples of Mission Statements

> I always had the feeling that I was born to do something. . . . I'm convinced that God has given me the talent, and I'm just trying to be patient with it.
>
> Carl Lewis
> world-class sprinter and long jumper

> I loved jumping so much because I could do it so well. Something was coming from deep down inside me. . . . I had something positive to do.
>
> Bob Beamon
> Olympic gold medalist and world-
> class long jumper

> I wanted that incredible feeling of being in command of myself that I get from pushing my body to the outer limits.
>
> Anonymous

LONG-TERM GOAL STATEMENT   Phase Two

Time: One 15-minute session

Benefits: This exercise will clarify your goal and its inherent rewards.

Distinctly different from your mission statement is the long-term goal. This goal serves as a major stepping-stone leading toward the eventual expression and *actualization* of your personal philosophy. If, for example, you are a recreational runner, your long-term goal might be to attain the ability to run comfortably and well, a stepping-stone leading to the actualization of a mission of taking responsibility for promoting and maintaining personal health and achieving a sense of well-being. If you're a college athlete, your long-term goal might be to qualify for a particular team, thus establishing a stepping-stone for *actualizing* your mission of becoming an integral part of a precise group effort in athletics. If you're an Edwin Moses, your long-term goal might be to win another Olympic gold medal, and success would represent a major step toward *actualizing* your mission—"To maintain my position as the best 400-meter hurdler in the world."

As you work to define your long-term goal, keep in mind that the information you now have from Lesson 1 is invaluable resource material. The long-term goal you choose should embody those athletic experiences you find intensely satisfying and for which you feel a strong desire to experience again. If you are not certain how your current goal reflects your volitional aspirations, make a cluster, following the instructions in Lesson 1, and explore this subject further.

As you think about your long-term goal, you should feel yourself becoming excited. You should feel that this goal is something you want very much to achieve. You should also feel that accomplishing this goal will greatly contribute to *actualizing* your sense of mission. You may feel that committing yourself to this long-term goal is taking a risk on your part, that it requires that you do something that is beyond what you presently know to be your limits. Remember that peak performers are, by their nature, educated risk-takers, and they know that engaging the risk itself becomes a source of excitement, with its own positive force for activating the powers of volition.

Your long-term goal should be clearly defined. Its definition should include a *timetable:* when you will initiate your plan to achieve your goal, and when you plan to achieve it. As you define this goal, be aware that rewards are an inherent factor; however, these rewards are always highly individualized. For example, winning a competitive event may be a reward desired by one person, while developing a new skill is the reward sought by another. On the included goal clarification form, you will rank the rewards inherent in your long-term goal according to their importance or priority to you.

When defining your long-term goal, keep in mind that your performance will be influenced by the clarity of your goal statement. In a research report published in the *International Journal of Sports Psychology* in January 1970, sports psychologist and consultant Dimitrova stated that "the more clear and detailed the goal, the greater is the athlete's tolerance of fatigue and distractions."

This exercise for developing your long-term goal statement provides a format for goal clarification and the prioritization of that goal's rewards.

Preparation
Have ready a loose-leaf binder. Allow for fifteen minutes of uninterrupted time.

Instructions
Record the following in your loose-leaf binder:

1. Describe your long-term goal. Be sure to include the levels of performance you want to achieve (times, distances, any other quantifiable material).
2. In what ways do you feel that your long-term goal embodies your ultimate mission?
3. What are the inherent rewards associated with your goal? Arrange the following in their order of importance to you (most important first, least important last): Winning; Feeling better, stronger, having greater stamina; Developing new skills; Gaining experience in a particular event or activity; Learning about fellow athletes, teammates, or

competitors through reading, conversations, films, etc.; other (describe).

4. When will you begin your program to achieve this goal?
5. When will you achieve your goal?
6. List any other details you can think of, such as where you will be when you achieve your goal, who you will be with, the weather, time of day, how you will feel, and so on.

WHERE ARE YOU NOW?

Athletes and coaches often make the same error in goal-setting, one that often leads to frustration long before the goal is accomplished. This error is made when a goal is established *without* the athlete's present capabilities being taken into careful consideration.

When lacking a realistic assessment of personal capabilities, athletes will frequently make their first step in training far too ambitious. The result is not the extension of those limits, as one would desire, but instead is most likely frustration in one's efforts. For example, a recreational runner, presently running five miles a day, decides to train for a marathon. In the first week he tries to double his mileage. Although he succeeds in this stated goal for the first two days, he is too tired and sore on the third day to train. He then misses the following two days due to various discomforts and to the lack of enthusiasm that has resulted from his pushing himself too hard, too soon. Be your own best friend—avoid too much, too soon! Your objective is to develop your full potential, not to see how much you can take.

Effective goal-setting begins not by focusing on where you want to be several months from now, but on *where you are at the present time.* Only with this attitude is it possible to establish a realistic first step with goals that have a high probability of success. This principle of the present is incorporated throughout the Peak Performance Training Program. You must consistently plan a number of small steps, beginning from where you are now and taking you where you want to go. Each step must have a high probability of success and must provide an opportunity for further assessment of your performance progress. These points will be more thoroughly reinforced as we get into program planning. For now, this should sufficiently emphasize the importance of self-assessment.

INDIVIDUAL SPORTS REQUIREMENTS

Each sport has its own criteria as to required stamina, strength, technique, and so on. For example, weight lifters must train for fast, short-term, explosive physical exertions, while marathoners must train to ration out energy over a number of hours. In order to assess accurately your present limits in terms of those goals you wish to achieve, you will need to know and understand the criteria of your own sport. Specific information is available for every conceivable sport (though such information is, of course, outside the scope of this book). Do not overlook any potential resources, be they fellow athletes, coaches, books, magazines, films, weekend sports clinics, lectures, or other help. Some specific areas you will want to explore for developing maximum potential in your own sport include physical conditioning, mental training or conditioning, diet, rules of the sport, and strategy.

    The following assessment statement provides a format designed to help you in focusing upon where you are now in relation to each area of training that applies to your sport.

THE PEAK PERFORMANCE ASSESSMENT CHART   Phase Three

    Time: One 30-minute session

    Benefits: This provides a clear picture of your present abilities for use in planning training steps that will have a high probability of success.

Figure 2–1 PEAK PERFORMANCE ASSESSMENT CHART

Performance area	Method of measuring performance level	Present performance level
Running	Speed, daily distances, miles run each week	Avg. 8 min./mile, 5 mi./day, 30 mi./week
Stretching and warm-ups	Time spent warming up and which muscles are involved	5 min./day Calf, back, and abdominals
Sprint on flat terrain	Timed distance	Quarter-mile in 1 min., 21 sec.
Diet	Amounts of oils and animal fats consumed per week	Less than 2 lbs./week

In setting goals and planning training strategies, you will be focusing on performance requirements that can be observed or empirically measured. For example, a runner might choose to focus on speed, duration of a run, and aerobic conditioning, all of which can be readily measured. A basketball player might focus on all of these plus the number of baskets made in a specific number of attempts. A golfer might focus on distance and accuracy for each stroke.

Preparation
Use blank sheets in loose-leaf binder.

Instructions
Based on your knowledge of your own sport, what are its most essential performance requirements? That is, what are the abilities and skills necessary to succeed in your sport? List these on a separate sheet of paper in your loose-leaf binder. Be certain you are choosing those performance requirements you can easily measure by counting, timing, measuring, and so forth. Figure 2–1 is an example of how you might use a peak performance assessment chart to your best advantage.

Now prepare a complete assessment chart for yourself, making certain that you include the performance areas that apply to you.

In the next phase you will be developing a training plan using a process that incorporates material recorded in your long-term goal statement and peak performance assessment chart, so be sure that you have been thorough in preparing these before going on.

THE PROGRAM TRAINING PLAN   Phase Four

Time: Varied

Benefits: The training plan is your road map for guiding the you who can become a peak performer to achieving your ultimate athletic mission. Your training plan will help reduce distractions and fatigue along the way.

As you design a training plan to accomplish your athletic mission, there are two categories of performance levels you will be considering. These are training segments, which represent each performance area, such as diet, warm-up, physical conditioning, and mental training; and training steps, which you create as you divide each training segment into goals that have a high probability of success.

For a moment, take a look at the sample training plan (Figure 2–2). Reading down the chart, note the following:

> The variety of training segments (diet, stretching, and so on) and the division of each segment into steps.

Reading across the chart, note the following:

> Dates recorded for the start and completion of each step.
>
> A column for noting training segments.
>
> The column for noting the step number of each segment.

> These are all self-explanatory. The remaining three columns require some explanation:

Figure 2-2 THE PROGRAM TRAINING PLAN

Long-term Goal: _To run the Bay to Breakers_

Inherent Rewards: First _To finish in top 10_ ; Second _To develop new skills_ ; Third _To gain Experience_

Segments: _Diet, stretching exercises, physical training_

STARTING DATE	SEGMENT	STEP	PRESENT PERFORMANCE LEVEL	GOAL, OR DESIRED IMPROVEMENT	FINISH DATE	CHANGES IN PROGRAM
8-2-84	Diet	1	Eating 4 lbs. of meat per week	2 lbs. of meat per week, max.	8-16-84	
8-16-94	"	2	2 lbs. meat per week, maximum	1 lb. meat per week, maximum	9-15-84	
9-15-84	"	3	1 lb. meat per week	½ lb. meat per week	9-30-94	Broke Training!
9-30-84	"	4	½ lb. meat per week	0 meat per week	10-10-84	Repeat week
8-2-84	Stretching Exercises	1	5 minute warmups, mostly thighs, calves, and upper back	10 minute warmups, same sequence	8-12-84	Change dates
8-12-84	"	2	10 minute warmups, same sequence	Add 30 second sequence for abdominals	8-16-84	
8-15-84	"	3	10 minute warmups for thighs, calves, abdominals, and upper back	12 minute warmups of thighs, calves, abdominals, and upper back	9-10-84	
8-2-84	Physical Training	1	Running 3 mi/day; 4 times/wks, 8/min.mi.	4 mi/day; 4 times/wk, 8/min.mi.	8-30-84	
8-30-84	"	2	4 mi/day; 4 times/wk, 8 min.mi.	5 mi/day; 5 times/wk, 8 min.mi.	9-18-84	
9-18-84	"	3	5 mi/day; 5 times/wk, 8 min.mi.	5 mi/day; 5 times/wk, 7 min.mi.	9-29-84	

From Peak Performance by Charles A. Garfield with Hal Zina Bennett. Published by Jeremy P. Tarcher, Inc. © 1984 by Charles A. Garfield.

Present performance level. In this column, record your own assessment of your performance level at each step within each segment. In the first step of each segment, you will obtain this information from your peak performance assessment chart, which you have previously completed. Then, as you divide the segment into additional training steps, each having a high probability of success, the information recorded as the present performance level in each case will be the goal, or desired improvement, achieved in the step immediately preceding. This, of course, reflects the fact that you have accomplished your goal in the previous step.

Goal, or desired improvement. In this column you record the improvement you want to make in each training step. It is *both* a stated goal and the criterion for determining whether or not you have succeeded. It is therefore important to formulate each goal in terms of specific *performance that is measurable.*

Changes in program. In this column you acknowledge the importance of flexibility in your training plan. For example, if you are working on improving your diet and a holiday comes up, it is likely that you will be tempted to break training and overeat or indulge in foods that are restricted from your diet. Instead of feeling guilty about doing so, a response that can snowball into frustration and result in your loss of volition to maintain the training regimen for a number of days, you simply note that you have broken training and repeat the training week you have neglected.

The changes column also offers you a way of making corrections in your training plan or implementing alternatives when you have an injury or when other commitments temporarily take you away from your training routine.

If you discover that your goals for a particular step are either too challenging or not challenging enough, use the changes column to make adjustments, either up or down, to achieve a better balance between your present performance level and your goal or desired improvement.

Begin now designing your own training plan. The step-by-step instructions greatly simplify this process.

Preparation
Make copies of Figure 2–3 or get six photocopies of it made.

Instructions
Step One: Fill in the Top of the Chart
In the spaces provided, state your long-term goal, the rewards of that goal, and how you prioritize these rewards. Then identify the training segments, or performance areas, that you decide will contribute the most toward your attaining the goal. Consider your choices of segments carefully, especially if your time is limited, since some performance areas will contribute more to your success than others, even though they require the same investments of time. Keep in mind the Soviet research we discussed in the chapter "Soviet Shamans in Milan," which demonstrated that athletes on balanced regimens of both mental training and physical training showed significantly greater performance improvement than athletes putting more time into physical training. Knowing this, you might decide to use the time riding the bus to and from work to mentally rehearse your sport (see Lesson 4). This may even enable you to reduce the hours spent in physical training and then perhaps to use the time saved to introduce a more complete program of stretching exercises for increased flexibility.

Step Two: Record the Segments
Decide on the first segment, or performance area, that you wish to plan. It is best to begin with the first thing you will do as you start your day. In the sample chart (Figure 2–2), diet is recorded as the first entry in the segment column. Record a starting date, and record a step number for the first entry.

Step Three: Describe Your Present Performance Level
In the column provided, describe briefly your present performance level, referring to your peak performance assessment

Figure 2-3 THE PROGRAM TRAINING PLAN

Long-term Goal: _____

Inherent Rewards: First _____ ; Second _____ ; Third _____

Segments: _____

STARTING DATE	SEGMENT	STEP	PRESENT PERFORMANCE LEVEL	GOAL, OR DESIRED IMPROVEMENT	FINISH DATE	CHANGES IN PROGRAM

From *Peak Performance* by Charles A. Garfield with Hal Zina Bennett. Published by Jeremy P. Tarcher, Inc. © 1984 by Charles A. Garfield.

chart, if needed. Remember to describe your performance level in terms that are measurable, such as time, distance, duration, and times per week (see example in Figure 2–2).

Step Four: Design the Training Steps

Decide on an intermediate goal for each segment. For example, working on diet, you might choose to eliminate all meat, substituting skinless chicken and fish. The purpose is to reduce your intake of animal fat. Having decided on this goal, you realize you do not want to make a *sudden* dietary change since, in the past, extremely rapid changes did not prove to be successful. You decide to make your change gradually, over a period of several weeks. Select the steps that will be comfortable for you.

How great a change can you tolerate comfortably over a period of a week or ten days? Your answer provides a realistic guideline for designing training steps with a high probability of success. (See Figure 2–2 for examples of how these changes are scheduled.) Record the appropriate starting and finishing dates, as well as segment numbers for each entry.

Step Five: Plan Each Segment

Following the same process as used above, develop complete plans for each segment or performance area that you decide to include in your training. As you design each step, remember to focus on behaviors that can be measured, and design each step for a high probability of success. As you progress with your plan, note that the goal for the step just completed becomes the present performance level for the following step. Note that the steps within each segment are to be numbered separately, since they refer to the steps *within* each segment itself rather than to those for the overall plan. In most cases the segments will overlap in time. For example, you will be working on diet during the same time period in which you are working on stretching. Conflicts in planning will be rare, but plan carefully in order to avoid too many changes or too much new material at once.

Step Six: Allow for Changes

The last column in the chart serves as a safety valve, allowing you flexibility in your training. I have found that athletes often become discouraged if they break training in any one area—a discouragement that could carry over to other segments of their training. For example, a minor injury could prevent you from completing your usual daily run. A snowball effect frequently develops when this occurs, and you may soon slack off on warm-ups, mental training, and other areas that are really not dependent upon the injured body part. To combat this, use the changes column to record what has happened and describe an alternate plan to compensate for time lost due to the injury. Simply record why you need to change your original plan and describe what you will do instead—and then do it! It's as simple as that.

Step Seven: Make a Schedule

Transfer your completed training plan to a calendar, and keep it in a handy place. Be sure to transfer the starting and finishing dates for each training step.

VISUALIZING GOALS

The final element in goal-setting is the creation of mental images—first of your mission, and subsequently of each goal you have included in your training plan.

As long as your plan consists merely of words on paper, you will be using only the rational capacities of your brain, which functions best for language and logical thought processes. The limits of language for performance instruction have been the subject of extensive research, demonstrating that words are useful only insofar as they aid us in creating mental imagery.

In a report to the Fifth World Sport Psychology Congress in Ottawa, Canada, in 1981, sports psychologist Evelyn G. Hall and tennis pro Charles J. Hardy stated: "Too much verbalization can cause frustration and anxiety. Since abstract verbal phrases evoke no visual images, verbal instructions should be concise and relevant to the movement. A single correct image is worth more than tons of verbiage, which overloads and restricts the performer's mind."

At the Ottawa conference, I compared notes on goal-setting techniques with both Soviet and East German sports researchers. V. M. Melnikov, of the Soviet Union, presented data from Russian athletic research centers showing that clear and accurate mental imagery of desired actions was invaluable. Melnikov said that "the smaller the difference between imagery and actual movement, the lower the probability of errors in performance and the greater the opportunity to influence the process of learning."

Swedish sports psychologist Lars-Eric Unestahl has worked extensively with a technique he calls "hypnotic goal-programming." With this technique, athletes are taught to achieve a deeply relaxed mental state, similar to a hypnotic or meditative state, and then to create mental images of their goals. In 1978, Unestahl studied a group of Sweden's champion downhill skiers and found that the best achievers clearly visualized their performance goals before every run, and thus were invariably those who had highly developed skills in this form of goal-setting. Like Melnikov, Unestahl discovered the importance of accuracy and clarity in goal-setting, finding that the "best skiers seem to have better ability to experience the actual course visually."

The creation of accurate mental imagery for guiding your physical movements is only one element of the goal-setting process for Peak Performance Training. Another important aspect is how this form of goal-setting influences the you who chooses to become a peak performer. Goal-setting that incorporates imagery gives definite shape and direction to volition, which, as we learned in Lesson 1, is the "heart of the mind-body problem." We know that "every change in the mental-emotional state . . . is accompanied by an appropriate change in the physiological state." This holds true in case after case where mental imagery has been used to enhance the effectiveness of Peak Performance Training.

Rachel McLish, winner of every major body-building title

including the Women's World Body-building Championships and the Ms. Olympia title, made one of the most dramatic statements I have heard about visualization training. In an interview appearing in *Women's Sports,* she told writer Kim H. Kapin that she spends months mentally preparing herself for competition: "I visualize the blood surging through my muscles with every repetition and every set I do. When I pose I've got a mental picture of how I want to look. When you have that in your brain, the physical body just seems to respond. It's important to tell yourself you are good and you look wonderful."

My experience, both as an athlete and in working with other athletes at the Performance Sciences Institute, substantiates that the linear goal-setting process, which you have just completed, provides a solid foundation for creating accurate mental imagery each step of the way. Create these mental images for each performance goal, and be certain to focus on each set of images prior to actually performing each step. For example, before you do any stretching exercises, review your written description of the goal, or desired improvement, on your training plan. This information provides the language and phrases used for creating clear, precise mental images of yourself actually accomplishing your goal. The following exercise will help you execute this process.

TRANSLATING GOALS INTO MENTAL IMAGES   Phase Five

Time: One 30-minute session

Benefits: This exercise facilitates translating the language of goal-setting into mental images. Through these mental images, you can transform words into actions.

Since peak performers have mental images of their goals clearly visualized, activity-oriented goals will provide you with mental models for the athletic competence you want to achieve. When creating mental images, you must have realistic views of where you are in terms of present performance levels, a perspective already developed in your training plan. At any given moment your awareness of where you are versus where you want to go provides positive stress, a motivating stimulus that will help you bridge the distance between your *desire* for success and the eventual *actualization* of that reality.

Preparation
Have your completed training plan on hand for convenient reference. Work at a time when you will not be disturbed for at least thirty minutes.

Instructions

Step One: Live Your Long-term Goal
Basing your thoughts and feelings on your long-term goal, as recorded in your training plan, picture yourself as a peak performer, having already achieved that goal. For example, a bicyclist has recorded as his goal, "Riding my bike from coast to coast." He thinks about this and finally begins creating the following mental image:

> I see myself riding my bicycle across the country, averaging about 120 miles per day. My body feels fantastic as I ride, and I feel filled with a sense of having unlimited strength. I see myself *honking* up long mountain roads, spinning smoothly across hot deserts, challenged by rains when I come to the Midwest, always in perfect harmony with my bike, trusting my body even as I nudge it into completing another ten or fifteen miles at the end of a hard day. Then, at the end of the ride, 3,000 miles from home, I savor victory. The complete actualization of a longtime dream, skyrockets going off in my head as I realize that I have actually done it, actually made this dream come true! I celebrate me and am filled with pride as I call friends, sharing this moment. It is sheer ecstasy.

Now create your own visualization, making clear pictures in your mind of how your victory will feel. Be sure to consider details such as what you will be doing and what you will be feeling. Focus on recalling your actions, emotions, and senses.

Do not allow yourself to be limited by memories of your past best performances. Although these can be inspirational, boosting the power of your volition, it is important for you to set your aspirations *extremely* high—not simply to aspire to repeat a performance level of the past. You are reaching into the future, not duplicating the past.

In particular, focus your attention on any physical sensations and emotions that you directly associate with the experience.

After completing your visualization, write down a brief description of it for future reference. It can be long and detailed, or short and abbreviated. The important thing is to make a written record that will trigger your full recollection of your visualization. Make a point of recalling your goal and re-creating this visualization in your mind at least once a day and a few moments prior to warm-ups when participating in an athletic event.

Step Two: Live Your Short Goals

Now, continuing the process as you did above, create mental images of your immediate goal and then of each step along the way to your long-term goal. The mental image you create should be clearly focused on the physical performance of that athletic improvement or change. For example, a runner is in training for her first marathon run, which she has learned will cover some extremely hilly terrain. After consulting with two other athletes who have previously run the course, she determines that her physical training should include working on an exercise machine to increase the strength of her legs. At her fitness center, she has her strengths and weaknesses evaluated, and from this designs her individualized training plan. After completing the first step of the plan (three sets, with eight repetitions each, of 170-pound leg presses), she is going on to step two (increasing the weight to 180 pounds). The following is her visualization:

> I see myself standing in front of the machine. The weights are set at 170 pounds, which I successfully pressed my last time around. I pull the pin on the weight rack and then insert it at the 180-pound mark. Then I walk around to the front of the machine and take my place on the seat. I take several deep breaths, feeling more relaxed and ready to lift as I do. I place my feet on the pedals. I grip the handles under the seat firmly with my hands. I inhale, hold my breath for a moment, then I press with my legs. I exhale as the weights rise smoothly and effortlessly. When the weights reach the top I say "one" to myself. I ease the weights down, inhaling as I do. I fill my lungs, press again, say "two" to myself, and slowly ease the weights down. I inhale. . . .

She creates mental images that take her through eight repetitions. Though it is not necessary to write down all eight repetitions, those athletes who excel in their sports do make *complete* visualizations of what they do, even for each of the repetitions in all exercises. As we have seen, Unestahl's research with Sweden's top downhill skiers showed that those athletes with the most complete goal visualizations did best both in time and in execution of movements. Similar findings were reported by Soviet sports psychologist Vladamir Kuzmin at the Fifth World Sport Psychology Congress in Ottawa. Kuzmin cited evidence gathered over twenty years, through working with more than 600 athletes, that showed the positive effects on performance when goals were visualized completely and vividly.

The goal image should be created for the specific step on which you are working at any given time. In other words, do not create images of step four of a segment when you have just begun step three. Jumping too far ahead in visualizing can create imprecise images and lead to discouragement, in the same way that making too great a jump in physical training can do. Remember the principle that each goal must have a *high probability of success.*

SUMMARY

Most visualization techniques found to be successful in Soviet training are extremely detailed and almost always duplicate the exercise itself in every sequence of movements. Although Soviet and East German sports research is not readily available for study by Westerners, a number of researchers of other nationalities (such as Unestahl, coaching professor Brent Rushall, and myself) have succeeded in duplicating the research results described at numerous conferences by Soviet and East German sports psychologists.

There is evidence that impressionistic mental imagery with many nuances of emotion is most effective for broad, long-term goals. On the other hand, short-term goals (such as those outlined in the steps of your training plan) are most effective when expressed as detailed, performance-oriented visualizations. The latter, in addition to providing high volitional stimulus, provide mental models for the actual activity. Keep these distinct differences in mind as you create the mental imagery of your own mission and goals.

Creating mental imagery as the final step in goal-setting leads us to the Soviets' most powerful mental training technique, which they term mental rehearsal. Mental rehearsal is a process that begins with learning the technique of deep relaxation, which will be the subject of Lesson 3.

APPLICATIONS FOR THIS LESSON OUTSIDE SPORTS

Career/Business: Just as athletes use goal-setting to formulate orderly and reasonable progressions toward the attainment of a particular goal, so in business can major changes be instituted with goal-setting. In recent years there has been a great deal of interest in the art of goal-setting, with the realization that if properly applied, it is a powerful technique for implementing positive, orderly change within an organization. Goal-setting techniques have been developed to a high level and have been applied in a variety of ways in everything from management development to sales programs in large corporations. Whether your goal is career planning and advancement, increasing sales, increasing productivity, reorganizing a department, or developing an idea for a new product or service, your skill in handling the goals of your project can make or break you. For example, if the long-term goal is not broken up into increments wherein success can be both measured and experienced by everyone whose labors contribute to the achievement of that goal, the task may seem overwhelming or unattainable to all concerned, and, thus, motivation is destroyed. On the other hand, if short-term goals or increments are not sufficiently challenging to the people who must carry them out, these people may think of their work as petty or they may feel that no discernible change or progress is being made toward a stated long-term goal. The results are that they lose interest, motivation disappears, and commitment to the project dies.

With sport as your metaphor (even if you are only a spectator), it is relatively easy to grasp the art of goal-setting, striking a balance between goals that are too challenging and those that are not challenging enough. Carefully assess, with every long-term goal, where you are now and where you want to go. Then, as I've described in the lesson you've just completed, break down the distances you must travel into increments that each promise a high probability of success. In this way, you can design a course of change and progress wherever you choose.

Personal: In personal health and self-improvement, the changes one desires may seem so large or elusive that one is frustrated before making the first step. For example, in starting a weight-loss program, the thing that defeats most people is this: they decide they want to look thin and trim but looking at their reflection in the mirror they see a bulging waistline and become discouraged. The mirror image seems painfully remote from their idealized self-image, and every time they look at a mirror they are reminded of how far from their ideal they are. Since it may take months to lose, let's say, fifteen pounds, the number of times a person will look in the mirror and see that discouraging, bulging waistline is immense.

Through goal-setting, however, one learns to measure progress not by comparing where they are now with the final goal but by dividing the journey toward that goal in measurable increments. For example, by setting incremental goals of losing, let's say, two pounds per week for seven weeks, progress is measured not against a seemingly remote ideal but against a weekly goal with a high probability of success. Motivation and commitment stay high because the person can measure progress and see positive proof that his or her efforts are worthwhile.

The same goal-setting techniques I describe here have aided thousands of people in starting exercise programs, making attitudinal changes, learning stress reduction, changing diet, improving marital relationships, and so forth.

Lesson 3

VOLUNTARY RELAXATION

Developing the Primary Skill for Controlling
Concentration and Physical Intensity

Every change in the physiological state is accomplished by an appropriate change in the mental-emotional state.

Elmer and Alyce Green
Beyond Biofeedback

In Soviet athletic training programs, two key skills must always be mastered. The first is the skill of voluntary relaxation—that is, the ability to relax the body consciously and put the mind in a quiet receptive state. The second skill is the ability to produce and creatively manipulate mental images. This is the process frequently referred to as "visualization." In Lesson 3, you will be learning to master the first skill, relaxation. The work on acquiring the skill of mental imagery will be presented in Lesson 4.

WINNING THROUGH RELAXATION:
THE ATHLETIC BENEFITS

In the 1970s, Stanley Krippner, Ph.D., former president of the Saybrook Institute of San Francisco, traveled to the Soviet

89

Union to study their research on the development of human "hidden reserves," or what Krippner called "latent human possibilities." In Alma-Ata, the capital of the Kazakh Republic of Russia, he was able to study the research of leading sports psychologist Alexander Romen. In his book, *Human Possibilities,* Krippner concluded that Romen's mental training methods were successfully used to "combat anxieties and fears, to imbue the athlete with confidence, to 'role-play' successful competition, to prevent 'prestart fever' and nervousness, and to provide athletes with a way to rest deeply before and between meets." In addition, Krippner reported that through the combined use of relaxation and mental imagery, athletes were able to "accelerate their reaction times" and also to "relieve fatigue" between events or plays.

Romen's work also demonstrated that the long tradition of tight-jawed determination and dedication to the single-minded goal of beating the competition is an attitude stereotyped in Western athletics (and colorfully expressed in Vince Lombardi's now famous statement, "Winning isn't everything, it's the *only* thing!"), and is indicative of an important but long overlooked *limiting* factor in athletics.

This attitude of blind, rigid determination is *not* the key that will allow you to develop your greatest strengths and maximize your human potential in sport. In fact, it will limit you from developing your human potential. Romen and his associates discovered this through their early experiments with the martial arts. They learned about the reserves of human energy—called *ki* in Japan, *prana* in India, and *chi* in China— and the skills for gaining access to these reserves, which make it possible to achieve sometimes miraculous physical accomplishments in judo, karate, and similar disciplines.

The Russians learned how to gain access to these high levels of human energy not through a get-tough posture of tight-jawed determination, but through the practice of rather subtle methods of breath control, mental concentration, and mind-body unification, which they learned by mastering ancient meditation techniques.

At the outset, the Soviets had some difficulty with meditation, since it was associated with religious practices that are not condoned by their government. This problem was circumvented, however, when it was found that the mechanism that made these meditation techniques effective in sports was *not* a mysterious process accessible only to those who followed particular religious traditions; instead, the mechanism was found in a state of relaxation that had been known to the medical profession for years. Romen and the other Soviet researchers discovered that the same results achieved in the martial arts through meditation could be attained using deep relaxation systems developed by German psychiatrist and neurologist Johannes H. Schultz of Berlin and by American physician Edmund Jacobsen.

Romen's adaptation of these relaxation systems brought to the Western sports arena the tradition of mental training that had served well in the martial arts for thousands of years. The significance of the Soviets' contribution in this area was perhaps best stated by Krippner after he had reviewed the evidence presented to him by the Russians, demonstrating how they were using self-regulation of the so-called autonomic functions in medicine, education, psychology, and athletics. Krippner spoke of "the value of self-regulation—a process through which individuals may gain greater control over their own functioning. The work of Alexander Romen thus serves as an important key, opening the door to the development of human potentials."

Interestingly enough, research in this field overlapped in the U.S.S.R. and the United States—although the Americans, for unknown reasons, were reticent about publicizing their work. For example, at about the same time that Romen was systematizing his study of these phenomena in the U.S.S.R., serious scientific inquiry into the claims of yogis who were able to alter their heart rates and other physiological functions was being conducted by Elmer and Alyce Green in the United States (see Figure 3–1). It was partially through my knowledge of the Greens' early work that I was able to be mentally receptive to the Soviets' reports of Romen's experiments. The Greens' work had not been applied directly to athletics, but the implications of that possibility had intrigued me.

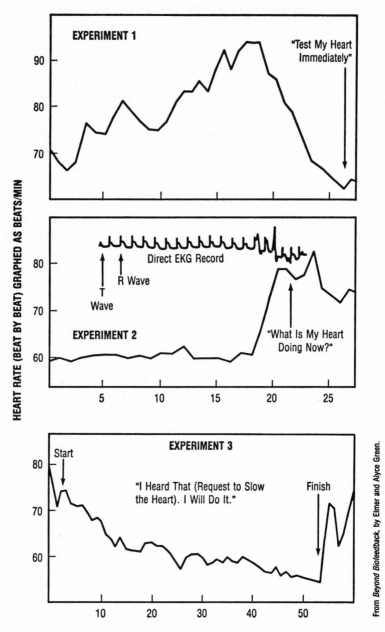

Figure 3–1 Electroencephalograms Showing Voluntary Control of Heat Rate. The above three charts show the subject's ability to change his heart rate at will. In the top chart, the subject, an Indian yogi, drops his heart rate from 97 beats per minute to 63 beats per minute. In the next chart, he raises it from 60 to a high of 82. In the bottom chart, he is asked to lower his heart rate from 73 down to 56 beats.

EMOTIONS AND PHYSICAL ACTION

Sports researcher and psychologist James E. Loehr, reporting in *Sports* journal, wrote that "an athlete's level of performance is a direct reflection of the way he or she feels inside" and that performing "toward the upper range of one's potential is a natural consequence of the right kind of internal feeling." Loehr's research demonstrates that the emotions an athlete may experience—whether prior to a game, during the competitive situation itself, or while anticipating an effort to break a personal record—are manifest in the nervous system and musculature as tension. Loehr believes these tensions can be monitored and regulated through the relaxation skills taught by the Soviets.

Demonstrating the links between emotions and muscular responses, American physician Edmund Jacobsen showed as early as 1942 that when a person does nothing more than imagine himself running, subliminal stimulation of the same muscles used in running can be electronically detected. One implication of this discovery pertains to fear. Once activated, fear can be responsible for a broad range of physiological responses (see Figure 3–2). These responses can then become entangled with or even override the more subtle learned signals that are required to execute most movements in sports. The powerful stimuli to get ready to fight or to run, which can be triggered by a wide range of emotions that may or may not be recognized as fear, may be, in fact, the polar opposites of the responses needed to do well in a sporting event. As David R. Kauss, professor at the School of Medicine, University of California at Los Angeles, and a lifelong student of the psychology of athletics, wrote in his book, *Peak Performance:*

> Fear . . . involves a physiological response as well as the recognition of the fear itself. Your body is built to respond almost immediately in emergencies, and this "fight-or-flight" reaction is provoked by a rush of adrenaline that activates your entire body. Obviously, this can be an excellent source of arousal, but the problems of dealing with the negative aspects of the fear arise equally quickly and dramatically.

Figure 3–2   HOW THE FIGHT-OR-FLIGHT RESPONSE AFFECTS
VARIOUS ORGANS OF THE BODY

Organ	Effect of Stimulation
Eye: Pupil	Dilation
Ciliary muscle	None
Gastrointestinal glands	Vasoconstriction
Sweat glands	Copious sweating
Heart: Muscles	Increased activity
Coronaries	Vasodilated
Systemic blood vessels:	
Abdominal	Constricted
Muscle	Dilated
Skin	Constricted or dilated
Lungs: Bronchi	Dilated
Blood vessels	Mildly constricted
Gut: Lumen	Decreased peristalsis and tone
Sphincters	Increased tone
Liver	Glucose released
Kidney	Decreased output
Bladder: Body	Inhibited
Sphincter	Excited
Blood glucose	Increased
Basal metabolism	Increased up to 50 percent
Mental activity	Increased
Adrenal medullary secretion	Increased

Adapted from *Physiology of the Human Body*, by Arthur C. Guyton, p. 231.

The main problem in using fear as a source of energy is that it tends to completely dominate the mind, making other, necessary thought processes next to impossible.

Romen believed that the athlete could use relaxation skills to control these negative reactions associated with fear. At the positive and opposite pole from fear is *confidence,* the importance of which was discussed in Lesson 1. Bud Winter, the track coach at San Jose State University for thirty years, coached athletes who went on to set a total of thirty-seven world records. He saw relaxation as one of the most powerful skills he had to teach. He felt that *confidence* is the antidote for the kinds of fear that athletes must confront and that "relaxation feeds confidence."

Romen showed that a number of significant changes occur, both in the body and in the mind, while a person is in a deeply relaxed, or meditative, state. Similarly, the Greens' research showed that during relaxation brain waves slow (as measured on an electroencephalograph, see Figure 3–3), heart rates slow, respiration rates slow and become rhythmic and even, and blood vessels throughout the body dilate, bringing an even, healthy flow of nutrients to every muscle cell. The opposite of deliberate, goal-oriented control (the Vince Lombardi school of thought), most frequently manifested in the fight-or-flight reflex, wherein only specific areas of the body are activated, the relaxed state allows the entire organism to find its "own optimal homeostatic balance," write the Greens. In this state the functions of body and mind are totally integrated. James Loehr has said that when this relaxed balance is achieved, one may note not only improved physical performance but an inner feeling of unity and confidence and a definite, enhanced sense of pleasure.

Loehr interviewed superathletes and assembled a composite of their statements, providing a picture of the relationships between relaxation and optimal sports performance: "I felt physically very relaxed, but really energized and pumped up. I experienced virtually no anxiety or fear, and the whole experience was enjoyable. I experienced a very real sense of calmness and quiet inside, and everything just seemed to flow automatically. . . . Even though I was really hustling, it was all very effortless."

Sportswriter John Jerome calls such moments "sweet spots." The feelings of *glory* or *transcendence* that athletes report derive from their ability to attain a high level of efficiency in their physical movements, a level of performance that requires complete harmony and cooperation between body and mind. I have found that when athletes are hitting their sweet

Seconds

0   1   2   3   4   5

100 microvolts   Beta

A. Start of Training Session

When a person is active with eyes open, the EEG record from a scalp electrode at the back of the head generally shows the presence of beta waves. 13 to 26 cycles per second, or higher (as shown in "A" record above).

Alpha and Beta

B. 2 Minutes Later

When the eyes are closed and the body is relaxed, alpha waves at 8 to 13 CPS often begin to appear. When alpha first appears it is sometimes a bit ragged from mixture with beta (see B).

Alpha

C. 10 minutes

As times passes, alpha often becomes smooth and regular in frequency, though of fluctuating amplitude (as in C).
When the body is deeply relaxed and a person becomes drowsy, theta waves at 4 to 8 CPS are often seen (as in D).

Theta

D. 15 minutes

In meditators, a smooth theta pattern (rather than ragged, as in D) is often associated with a quiet body, quiet emotions, and a quiet mind, but consciousness does not diminish.

Theta

E. 20 minutes

At this stage, which is hinted at in E, one can begin to "become conscious of the unconscious." If the subject goes to sleep, irregular delta waves at 1 to 4 CPS begin to be seen (as indicated in F).

Delta

F. 25 minutes

From *Beyond Biofeedback*, by Elmer and Alyce Green.

Figure 3–3 Brain-Wave Patterns While Consciously Inducing a State of Deep Relaxation. The above data were obtained from the strip-chart record of a subject using biofeedback techniques to induce a state of deep relaxation. It shows the progressive slowing of mental activity as relaxation is fully achieved.

spots, their skill levels are higher and their motions quicker, more accurate, and more powerful.

Many athletes have experienced such moments, moments when everything comes together exactly right and every movement is fluid, sure, and natural; at such times, the athlete is completely free from consciously thinking about what he or she is doing. It is as though they were being directed by a power much greater than themselves, all the physical energy and information they needed mysteriously transmitted to every muscle cell in their bodies. It is not unusual for the athlete's sense of unity and power to be extended, in the mind, to the external environment. In his book *The Four-Minute Mile,* runner Roger Bannister described just such a moment: "No longer conscious of my movement, I discovered a new unity with nature. I had found a new source of power and beauty, a source I never dreamt existed." Basketball champion Patsy Neal has said that there are moments "that go beyond the human expectation, beyond the physical and emotional ability of the individual. Something *unexplainable* takes over and breathes life into the known life. One stands on the threshold of miracles."

Sometimes these moments result in important victories, such as taking an Olympic medal or completing a winning play in the Superbowl, but just as often they are but brief moments in time, meaningful solely to the individual athlete—a single putt in eighteen holes of golf, five minutes during a four-mile run, a sequence of serves in a whole hour of racquetball. Once such a moment has happened, an athlete will go to great lengths to repeat that experience. This quest becomes what psychologist William Glasser called a *positive addiction*—"a trancelike, transcendental mental state" that athletes seek as avidly as they seek awards and personal or world records.

THE RIGHT BRAIN IN SPORTS

To fully understand the role played by relaxation in the mental training of athletes, we need to turn to recent research concerning the human brain and the nature of human consciousness. Here we learn that the right and left hemispheres of the brain, in addition to having a certain degree of autonomy, also exhibit a distinct division of labor. In his book *The Right Brain*, T. R. Blakeslee stated that the left hemisphere specializes in *linear* and *logical* processes, such as language, math, and so on. The right hemisphere is described as *intuitive,* specializing in spatial problems and in the creation of mental images. Because of these characteristics, it is the right brain that is best suited to direct athletic activity. In an article entitled "Using the Right Brain in Sports," sports psychologist Evelyn Hall and tennis pro Charles Hardy wrote: "Many of the complex movements inherent in sport cannot be adequately expressed in verbal terms. In sport, much of the action involves manipulating and rearranging mental images."

Hall and Hardy added that in most sports the athlete clearly uses both hemispheres, but that *dominance* may change. For example, with right hemisphere dominance, images are produced that direct the nervous system in the business of moving the muscles; with left hemisphere dominance, logical problems can be solved, such as game strategy. Problems arise when the athlete attempts to control physical responses with the left brain, in the form of verbal criticism or orders. In Timothy Gallwey's book called *The Inner Game of Tennis,* we learn that when the left brain is engaged, the right loses its influence, and that the result is frustration, anxiety, or inadequate physical movement. Gallwey's system addresses the issue of hemispheres, but expresses these as "Self 1" (left hemisphere) and "Self 2" (right hemisphere). The principle of Gallwey's system is to suppress the verbal Self 1 and to encourage the visualizing Self 2 to dominate and direct the athletic movement.

While Gallwey sees the solution as being largely a matter of disciplining yourself so that you do not activate Self 1, the Soviets have recognized that the problem goes much deeper than this. Although Gallwey's system clearly works in recreational situations, some athletes report that it tends to work less well in high-competition circumstances. Alexander Romen's work shows that in stressful situations one may get locked into the left hemisphere dominance, using the verbally skilled portion of the brain to "figure out" a solution to the problem causing the stress. For many, this is apparently part of the fight-or-flight response. When the left brain takes over, physical movements become more clumsy and/or inaccurate.

According to Romen, relaxation training provides you with a highly dependable skill for subduing left brain activity even while you are heavily stressed. Where Romen and Gallwey differ is not in the principles of their systems, but in the depth and completeness of the mental training programs they prescribe.

A study published by C. M. Cade and N. Coxhead in their book *The Awakened Mind* of some 3,000 meditators with relaxation skills comparable to those learned by Soviet athletes (and which you can develop through the exercises in this chapter) showed that these meditators had developed a more integrated balance and control of the two hemispheres of the brain than was demonstrated in the same tests on nonmeditators. This process of relaxation produces a sense of mind-body integration, a state of mind that sports psychologists have noted as characteristic of superathletes.

In addition, those who have mastered the art of relaxing under pressure have an ability to control anxiety and other emotional responses (this will be discussed in Lesson 5). The same deep relaxation techniques (meditation) that for thousands of years have allowed Eastern people of wisdom to still their verbal thoughts and tap into nonverbal consciousness (right hemisphere dominance) are now being shown to be effective in sports (see Figure 3–4). A number of superathletes, including Joe Namath, Billie Jean King, Bill Walton, Jack Nicklaus, Jane Blalock, and O. J. Simpson, have used meditation and various other relaxation systems for improving their performances in competition.

Reflecting on the differences between Eastern and Western sports training, educator James L. Hickman wrote in an article entitled "How to Elicit Supernormal Capabilities in Athletes," "Western athletes frequently experience spontaneous bursts of energy that contribute to exceptional performances.

Figure 3–4 EXTRAORDINARY HUMAN CAPABILITIES IN YOGA AND SPORT

Yogin Accomplishment	How It Translates to Sport
Exceptional control of bodily functions, emotions, thoughts, imagination, etc.	Pulse, heart rate, breathing, and other vital functions come under the control of the runner doing a marathon, or of an underwater swimmer holding his breath at times for more than five minutes and/or at depths exceeding forty feet, or of a race-car driver making the hairpin turns that ordinarily cause dizziness and loss of equilibrium.
Mastery of physical and mental pain	Dissociation from pain in football, boxing, wrestling and other sports in which breaks, sprains, and other injuries are frequent. Concentration is so great that athletes suffering such injuries are often completely unaware of them until after the game has ended.
Ability to survive with little oxygen	Anaerobic abilities exercised by ocean divers and long-distance runners.
Ability of Tibetan monks to generate heat from within their bodies with little or no muscular movement	Sailors, mountain climbers, and swimmers report abilities to withstand freezing temperatures with little or no discomfort.
Levitation	Similar mechanisms exercised when martial-arts practitioners make themselves heavier or lighter through manipulation of *ki* energy. Lee Evans and other sprinters talk of "tipping"—a spontaneous lifting sprint form that seems to carry the runner on the tips of his toes as if he were hardly touching the track.
The ability to go without sleep	Restoration of energy between meets by employing deep-relaxation systems.
Eternal youth	George Blanda was a starring player for the Oakland Raiders at 45; Sam Snead was a money-maker on the PGA tour at 65; track and swimming records for people over 40 are falling at incredible rates.
Precognition	Football player David Meggyesey made many tackles, he says, because he could foresee the moves of the opposing teams before the play began; similar experiences have been reported by players in football, basketball, hockey, and soccer.

Figure 3–4 (*Continued*)

Yogin Accomplishment	How It Translates to Sport
Telepathy	Extraordinary power of communication between team members, with which one member can foresee what another will do in a play.
Control of other people through manipulation of their physiological functions, their thoughts and feelings, etc.	The ability to psyche out opponents. Muhammad Ali and Jim Brown were notable in this.
Heaviness and immovability	Getting in touch with one's *ki* energy in the martial arts allows one to seem to become heavier and more difficult for an opponent to lift or move. Football players and wrestlers also talk about this power.
Extraordinary strength and endurance, as with *lung gom* walkers who walk for weeks, without stopping, through the mountains of Tibet	The endurance of marathon runners and the extraordinary bursts of strength that sometimes occur in weight lifting, boxing, wrestling, and other sports.

Adapted from *The Psychic Side of Sports*, by Michael Murphy.

The Eastern martial arts, however, teach techniques to develop reserves of energy."

It was Alexander Romen's discovery of the techniques for teaching the athlete how to gain voluntary access to the peak performance state, not the invention of those techniques *per se,* that won Romen and the Soviets their place in sports history.

The key ingredient of Romen's work is a mental training exercise for creating deep relaxation. In this training process, the subject is taught to voluntarily induce specific feeling states. These states are associated with physiological changes such as heart and respiration rates, blood flow, and body temperature.

According to Romen's research, deep relaxation is achieved by learning to produce four feeling states:

1. Inner calm and muscular relaxation throughout one's body, along with a free rhythm of breathing and clear sensations of heaviness and immobility.

2. Feelings of warmth in the arms, legs, abdomen, chest, and head.

3. Feelings of coolness in separate parts of the body, and the simultaneous contrasting sensations of warmth in other parts.

4. Feelings of a calm heart with strong, even, steady heartbeats.

The Greens, in their tests of the same autogenic training techniques, measured respiration, heart rate, galvanic skin response, blood flow, and temperature in the hands. During the part of the exercise in which the subject was asked to imagine his hands becoming warmer, the Greens measured a corresponding increase in hand temperature of 10°F during a two-minute period, which was consistent with Romen's findings. Additional experiments convinced the Greens that the use of the imagination to induce a feeling of warmth, both in the hands and feet, brought about "vasodilation" (increase in the capacity of the blood vessels), with a measurable increase in blood flow to those areas of the body to which the subject directed his attention.

In a report on a typical subject undergoing the test for the effectiveness of autogenic training (in this case, a woman suffering from hypertension), Elmer Green stated that such training "gave her the ability to turn off chronic tension in the sympathetic nervous system (the 'fight-or-flight' system) and helped her develop a more relaxed style of living." Green concluded that "when a person learns to warm the hands, vascular relaxation and rebalancing often occur over the entire body."

Learning to warm the hands brings about changes in the brain and nervous system as well. The pressures of normal living activate the sympathetic nervous system, resulting in defense responses characterized by the fight-or-flight response. This activation triggers an increase in blood pressure and heart rate and a general activation of nerve cells and muscle fibers throughout the body. Often, tension levels in the sympathetic nervous system fail to drop, or normalize, after activation—

that is, after a confrontation with another person, an aggravating wait in rush-hour traffic, and so on. The tension level may then become *chronic*—that is, subliminal muscular activation is going on all, or most, of the time. However, as one learns to relax through autogenics or any other deep relaxation technique, the chronic or habitual pattern of tension diminishes, freeing the person of those habits of feeling and behaving and releasing energy that can be directed to athletic excellence. There is, as the Greens have reported, a "decreased activation in the sympathetic nervous system," allowing the individual to exercise more choice in the ways he or she uses energy.

In working with athletes, I tell them to look upon the fight-or-flight response as a stereotypical behavior pattern and a potential enemy of the subtler, learned responses associated with their sports. When activated by worry, fear, or trauma, this *automatic* response, even at its subtlest levels, can obscure or even cancel the more precise, *learned* program of athletic coordination and movement. In this respect, the effects of the intrusion of the fight-or-flight response in sports can be compared to what would happen if a simply programmed automatic pilot (a program designed to maintain a very simple and particular flight path) was accidentally activated while the human pilots were attempting to guide a plane through a complex and dangerous maneuver that required their quick responses. Because it would fail to respond to the conditions of the present, the automatic pilot would cause the plane to crash.

As powerful as the inborn fight-or-flight program may be, we are not at its mercy. The reason for this is complex: first, although the program for the response is automatic, the perception that triggers it is not, according to the Greens. The perception is learned and is, to a large extent, subject to alteration. The ability to relax even in the face of what most people would perceive as a threat or danger allows the well-trained athlete to choose between his "automatic pilot" and the more appropriate program learned through years of athletic training. Julius Menendez, who coached Muhammad Ali in the 1960 Rome Olympics, was interviewed by Bud Winter for the latter's book *Relax and Win*. Menendez spoke of the champ's extraordinary ability to relax under pressure and counted this as one of Ali's top assets, saying that in high-level competition, where there is a lot of pressure, this can be the difference between winning and losing—the mark of a champion.

THE SECOND WIND

For centuries it has been claimed that yogis could get along with little or no sleep. The question naturally arose that if meditation allowed the yogis to reduce requirements for vital sleep, might relaxation be applied by the athlete for rejuvenating and refreshing him- or herself between fatiguing athletic events or plays? Could relaxation be used for creating the so-called second wind in the midst of play?

The need for sleep is not fully understood by scientists, but the Soviets believe that it is a period of time in which the brain cells are restored. Ivan Pavlov believed that the cells of the cerebral hemispheres are exceptionally sensitive and subject to damage from excessive stress and strain. Protection is provided them by what he called the *inhibitory* processes of sleep, which for a time block outside stimuli, allowing the cells to mend. It was Pavlov's contention that sleep is an internal inhibitor that radiates throughout our bodies, extending over both hemispheres of the brain as well as to the lower brain centers.

In this rejuvenating process of sleep, according to Pavlov, some restorative benefits could be expected from only *partial* inhibition of stimuli—as might be provided by deep relaxation. A number of Soviet researchers, including Romen and the educational psychologist K. I. Platonova, did extensive work on the effectiveness of relaxation without sleep in providing the inhibitory benefits ordinarily provided by sleep. In his review of the Soviets' research, Stanley Krippner concluded: "During the transition from wakefulness to sleep, or in such altered states of consciousness as those induced by hypnosis, suggestion, or relaxation, one part of the cortex may be in a state of sleep inhibition while the other part may be awake."

Brent S. Rushall, professor of coaching science at Lakehead University in Ontario, Canada, has said that "a rest period of concentrated relaxation would help the recovery process. It is particularly good for use between repetitive performances such as are required in gymnastics or between heats and finals."

Rest is, of course, a necessary bodily function, without which the athlete cannot hope to perform at optimal levels. But many athletes find it difficult to sleep prior to important athletic events, and knowing how important sleep is to their performance, they may become worried and tense because they know they are not getting what they require. *This increased anxiety may be even more detrimental to performance than the lack of sleep itself.* Rushall found that athletes who have learned an adequate relaxation program can use this skill both to get the rest they need and to reduce anxiety about their sleeplessness.

Rushall and Romen have both suggested that conscious relaxation is equal to, and in some cases even better than, sleep. Thus, the relaxation skills presented here will be helpful in producing restful periods that are essential for athletic preparation and also for rapid recovery during and following a stressful or fatiguing event.

RELAXATION AND THE ART
OF VISUALIZATION

As noted earlier, the Soviet athletic training programs are built around two key skills: relaxation and the creation of mental imagery. Relaxation is an essential first step to visualization and mental rehearsal. It creates an open, receptive state of mind necessary for the process of creating winning mental imagery, which will be presented in Lesson 4. For now, it is enough for you to know that development of the relaxation techniques in this chapter is necessary in order to successfully learn the skills to follow.

THE THREE PHASES OF RELAXATION TRAINING

Because of its importance in peak performance training, the relaxation program is presented in three phases. In Phase One, you will explore how tension and relaxation are manifest in your body and mind, utilizing techniques developed and broadly tested over many years by Edmund Jacobsen. Although this is a short, one-lesson exercise, it provides a solid reference point for understanding the subtle, muscular feelings associated with relaxation and tension. In Phase Two, through three twenty-minute training sessions, you will learn diaphragmatic breathing, which by itself will help you relax in ways both comforting and profound. In Phase Three, the knowledge you assimilate as you explore tension and relaxation as well as the basic skills you master in diaphragmatic breathing will be applied directly through autogenic training, which is presented in six steps. These steps may seem deceptively simple, and you may be tempted to move through the exercies too quickly. *Do not make this mistake!* While the *conscious* part of these exercises is simple, your body must undergo subtle changes, often at the subliminal level, before training is complete. Respect the fact that you are training parts of your musculature and nervous system that learn less quickly than your mind.

Many of the less comprehensive relaxation programs presented over the past few years have ultimately failed, not because their basic principles were wrong, but because a real "training effect" was not achieved. Until real change occurs within you—measured as your attainment of the ability to induce a deep state of relaxation *at will*—no lasting benefits can be derived from any such training system. This book is designed for athletes who want to make major changes in the skills and abilities they bring to the game and, for that matter, to life. When carefully followed, the training program presented here will not only allow you to eliminate old habits that are limiting your performance, but it will also vastly expand the range of mental skills at your disposal. It's like opening a door to a storehouse of abilities you may not even know you possessed.

Begin now with Phase One of the relaxation program, and you will soon discover for yourself the power of this skill.

EXPLORING RELAXATION AND TENSION Phase One

Time: One 20-minute session
Benefits: You will attain an awareness of tension and relaxation states.

Fifty years ago, Edmund Jacobsen developed a system for progressive relaxation that included more than 200 exercises. These exercises began with a series for teaching awareness of tension and relaxation as each is expressed in various muscle groups throughout the body. Jacobsen and others working with his system treated thousands of people with tension-related health complaints such as chronic pain, indigestion, ulcers, hypertension, and irregular heartbeat. Through his work, Jacobsen learned of the powerful links between the mind and body, and in particular the links between emotions and muscle.

Jacobsen believed that by fully relaxing the muscles, one could in turn relax the mind. His statement that "an anxious mind cannot exist within a relaxed body" should remind you of the Greens' statement that "every change in the physiological state is accompanied by an appropriate change in the mental-emotional state."

In teaching relaxation to large groups, I have learned that most people have individualized perceptions about what it means to feel relaxed. The use of the electroencephalograph often reveals a highly charged, active mind in people who believe they are fully relaxed; such people are often astounded to discover the degree of mental excitement they are manifesting when they believe they are fully relaxed. From observations of this phenomenon, Jacobsen and his associates concluded that, to be successful, any relaxation system must begin with exercises that teach an awareness of tension and relaxation.

In the following exercise, you will tense, and then relax, certain muscle groups. Once you explore how you feel with your muscles deliberately tensed and then relaxed, it is usually much easier to induce deep relaxation with the breathing and autogenic exercises that follow.

Preparation

Perform this exercise in a quiet place where you will not be disturbed for at least twenty minutes. With each step along the way, pause for two or three seconds to be aware of your sensations and feelings. This exercise is to be done slowly and quietly. You will achieve optimal benefit if you sit in a straight-backed chair, since an alert, upright posture maintains a spinal alignment close to that used in classic, time-tested meditative postures.

Instructions

Step One

Make a fist and squeeze firmly. Maintain the clenched position and trace your muscular involvement. Following only your feelings, and without using words, note the sensations in your palm and fingers.

Focus attention on the feelings in your wrist, the top of your hand, your forearm.

Take your time. Be attentive to every sensation, no matter how subtle or insignificant it may seem.

Again without using words, become aware of how your upper arm feels, your shoulder, your chest, your back.

How does your clenched fist affect your breathing? Your stomach muscles? Do you notice any tension, or any other sensations, in your pelvis? Buttocks? Lower back?

How do your legs feel? Do any sensations in your legs seem associated in any way with your fist?

Release your clenched fist. Let your hand relax. Shake it gently. Relax it. Shake it again. Relax it again.

Now clench your fist once more.

Make a mental note of any words that come to mind to describe the *sensations* you feel. Concentrate on your sensations as intensely as you can. To do this, use only single words to describe what you feel. Stop yourself if you have an impulse to find reasonable explanations for your feelings. Use single words only. Examples: *tight, contracted, prickly, hard, cold, strong, warm.* Responses are often highly individualized, and yours may or may not include any of the examples given.

Make a mental note of simple words that come to mind to describe any *emotions* you are feeling, particularly those associated with your fist. Examples: *resolute, fear, certainty, confusion.*

Now completely relax your fist. Let your arm hang loosely at your side. Mentally note any physical sensations you are feeling while in this relaxed position, again using single words only. Examples: *loose, light, tingling, warm.* Pay close attention to subtle sensations. Follow these sensations over your musculature as you did when clenching your fist.

Now go on to step two.

Step Two

All the sensations and single-word thoughts you noted as you clenched your fist are manifestations of the experience of tension. Similarly, the sensations and single-word thoughts you noted after relaxing your fist are manifestations of the experience of relaxation. For the moment, turn your attention to the sensations and the single words you used to describe them. *Feel* your body's responses. Do not try to define your experience or to draw any conclusions.

In future exercises, your memories of the sensations of tension and relaxation you have experienced here will be important. But do not try to memorize what you have experienced here—your impressions of the experience will be automatically stored in your neuromuscular system.

The following instructions will help you condense the experience and will give you a focus that will sharpen your ability to summon up this material:

Recall the experience of tension you felt as you made a fist. Say to yourself, "This is how the experience of tension feels."

Recall the experience of relaxation you felt as your relaxed your fist. Say to yourself, "This is how the experience of relaxation feels."

The more clearly you can recall and relive these experiences, first of tension and then of relaxation, followed by a statement naming that experience, the more complete will be your memories of these states. Whenever you read about tension or relaxation from now on, it will be the experiences that you have discovered in this exercise that we will be discussing.

BREATHING FOR PEAK PERFORMANCE Phase Two

Time: Three 20-minute sessions

Benefits: You will learn to control tension and how to induce relaxation under stressful conditions.

Most of us are taught to stand with our stomachs in and our chests out. Although this may be good for posture, it unfortunately inhibits full, diaphragmatic breathing. Air stays high in the chest and the lungs are never adequately filled. In the athletic world, this impedes performance.

Of all the relaxation skills, diaphragmatic, or belly, breathing is the easiest to learn, providing almost immediate feedback through the attainment of a soothing sense of relaxation that you can often feel throughout your body.

In full diaphragmatic breathing, the lungs are fully inflated, just as they are in newborn babies. The belly rises and falls, the diaphragm (the muscle separating the chest and abdominal cavities) stays loose and flexible, and breathing is rhythmic and sure. Animals in the wild are primarily "belly breathers," even when they are preparing for a kill or confronting an enemy.

Most people in modern society, however, are thoracic, or chest, breathers. This is associated with left brain domination and is a habit that has evolved in societies in which logical and analytical skills, rather than emotions, are highly valued. We have long observed that emotions are associated with the musculature of the abdomen; thoracic breathing tends to cut this area off. However important this breathing pattern may be in the socialization process, it must be changed for peak performance in sports. Diaphragmatic breathing is important here because it increases the amount of oxygen taken into the bloodstream and enhances right brain activity.

Proper diaphragmatic breathing involves the entire torso. To understand how it works, it is useful to envision this breathing pattern as a three-step process. First, the diaphragm moves downward, creating a vacuum in the chest cavity that draws air into the lower portions of the lungs. Next, the middle part of the lungs begin to inflate, and the abdominal area expands—from just below the rib cage to just above the navel. Finally, the chest itself expands, filling the upper portion of the lungs.

Learning to breathe deeply, as described in this exercise, is an integral part of mastering deep relaxation techniques. Since larger volumes of air are moved as you breathe deeply, breathing rhythms become slower and more steady. As Gay Hendricks pointed out in *The Centered Athlete,* "As we free our breath (through diaphragmatic breathing) we relax our emotions and let go of our body tensions. Proper breathing regulates basic physiological responses."

When angry, fearful, or tense, you pant, breathe less deeply, or even choke up, greatly reducing the volume of air you can take in to nurture brain and muscle cells throughout the body. Moreover, your heart rate accelerates. The consequences can sometimes be dramatic, ranging from slight fatigue to loss of physical coordination and mental concentration to, in the extreme, passing out under the pressure of competition. Learning to monitor and control your breathing gives you the ability to maintain appropriate rhythms, thus ensuring optimal oxygenation for proper brain- and muscle-cell efficiency.

In addition to increasing the amount of oxygen in the blood, there is considerable evidence that full diaphragmatic breathing strengthens weak abdominal and intestinal muscles. Furthermore, once you establish a habit of abdominal breathing, your heart rate will tend to decelerate. Mental concentration is increased and the ability to create mental imagery (which will be presented in Lesson 4) is greatly enhanced. Evidence for these broad changes has been cited by medical researchers, educational psychologists, and athletes.

Preparation

The first time you do this exercise, it is best to be lying down. Find a quiet place where you will not be disturbed for at least twenty minutes. *After you experience your breathing patterns and do the exercise at least three times in a quiet place, it will not matter where or under what circumstances you practice thereafter.* You can practice it at your desk at work, at home while watching TV, or while waiting to participate in a sports competition.

L. John Mason, in his book *Guide to Stress Reduction,* recommends that we *remind* ourselves to practice deep breathing, and he suggests that we associate it with something commonly done throughout the day. For example, if you work in a busy office, let the ringing phone remind you to breathe deeply. Don't answer the phone on the first ring, but let it ring a couple of extra times while you take a deep breath. Similarly, you might place a piece of tape on your watch, or on the clock on the wall, to remind yourself every time you check the time to take a deep breath. Ultimately, however, the first sign of stress in your life will be your signal to take a deep, refreshing diaphragmatic breath.

Instructions

Step One: Which Type of Breather Are You?

While lying on your back, place your hand high on your abdomen, just below the rib cage. Take a deep breath. As you do, notice the way your hand moves. Does it move up, down, not at all? If you are a diaphragmatic breather, your hand will move up. If you are a thoracic breather, your hand will move only slightly, if at all, or even down.

Watch your hand as you breathe. Be aware of where most of the movement occurs: your chest, upper abdomen, lower abdomen, or all three.

Step Two: Focus on Your Abdomen
Exhale, emptying your lungs completely.

Take a deep breath. As you inhale, place your hand on your abdomen and monitor the breathing pattern as follows:

Lower abdomen expands, creating a vacuum in the chest cavity, causing air to be drawn into the lower lungs.

As the middle section of the lungs fills, your upper abdomen expands.

While you continue inhaling, your chest then expands, filling the upper regions of your lungs.

Step Three: Learn How You Breathe
Exhale. Empty your lungs completely.

Take a deep breath. Do you inhale through your nose or through your mouth?

Exhale.

Do you exhale through your nose or through your mouth?

Mentally note your present breathing patterns before going on to the next step.

Step Four: Correct Your Breathing
Take a deep breath. This time, even if it is *not* your usual pattern, inhale through your nose, filling your lungs completely.

Exhale through your mouth; feel the warm air pass through your mouth and lips as you do.

Follow this routine whenever you are breathing for relaxation:

Inhale through your nose; exhale through your mouth.

Step Five: Put It All Together
Take a deep breath, inhaling through your nose.

Watch your body as, first, your lower abdomen expands, then your upper abdomen, and finally your chest.

Hold your breath for ten seconds.

Feel the tension build in your throat and mouth as you hold your breath.

Release your breath with a "sigh of relief," exhaling through your mouth.

At first, the sigh of relief may be uncomfortable, but try it several times until you can do it freely and comfortably. It is very beneficial, releasing muscle tension throughout your body.

AUTOGENIC TRAINING   Phase Three

Time: Two 15-minute sessions daily for three months

Benefits: You will attain the ability to relax body and mind at will. The same skill is used as an integral part of subsequent lessons.

In the early 1970s, the Soviet physician A. G. Odessky published a guide on autogenics for the general public. He noted that the term *autogenics* was derived from the Greek words *auto* and *genous,* and that these two root words together translated as "self-creation" or "self-generation." He wrote further, "Our training develops people's abilities to control consciously their various physiological processes—for example, to control digestion, breathing, blood circulation, metabolism, and also to control emotions, moods, and to sharpen attention."

Odessky explained that almost immediately after we master relaxation techniques, we are able to rid ourselves of the counterproductive emotions and sensations that tend to plague us as we head into competitive situations. He refers to his program as a system of "psychological gymnastics through which a person can attain a complete control of his psyche."

The key element of Odessky's program is a form of relaxation that he, Romen, and other Soviet researchers learned from Indian yogis and from the work of Johannes Schultz, whose techniques were applied as early as the 1930s in the treatment of diseases such as high blood pressure, digestive problems, and muscular-skeletal disorders.

Each step presented here should be mastered before going to the next. As emphasized before, this kind of training requires certain changes to occur in your mind and body that *do not come about instantly.* The process of change usually occurs in about the same amount of time as it does in an aerobic exercise program—that is, in about three months. Along the way, you will notice pleasant sensations in specific parts of your body. You may also notice an increase in your ability to concentrate on your game and other activities. Look for these changes as you gradually progress through the program.

The formulas you will learn for creating sensations of heaviness and warmth may also produce a pleasant, drowsy state. This is an indication that the exercise is working for you. However, you do not want to fall asleep while you are training, so if you have a tendency to nod off, try sitting in a straight-backed chair, leaning slightly forward as you do the exercise.

Each step begins with instructions to use deep diaphragmatic breathing, as you learned to do in the previous exercise. For this reason, it is necessary to be very comfortable with this form of breathing before you begin autogenic training. If you do not feel you have mastered diaphragmatic breathing, review the previous exercise. In addition, knowledge gained from the material earlier in this lesson on exploring relaxation and tension should be used here whenever you encounter the words *relaxation* or *tension.* When these words come up, recall the sensations you explored with the first exercise in this section.

The complete autogenic training program is presented in six steps. Spend approximately two weeks on each step, *except where noted otherwise. Don't rush yourself.* Learning in small increments is essential here. The exact time you spend will be determined by the complexity of the step as well as by your own learning speed. If some sessions take longer, do not be concerned; the important thing is to master each step to your complete satisfaction. Ideally, Odessky recommends planning two training periods per day, preferably one in the morning and one in the evening. Stick to a training regimen of at least five days per week, with never more than one day between sessions.

Review the entire exercise, *all six steps,* before you begin actual training. This will give you a clear overview of where you are going and what you will be doing. It will also provide you with a clear picture of your training goals and how you will want to pace yourself.

Preparation

In Odessky's program, the student assumes one of the three following positions. Choose whichever one is most comfortable for you.

1. *The Bench:* Sit in a straight-backed chair or on a bench, with both feet flat on the floor. Let your head hang slightly forward, with your hands and forearms resting loosely on your thighs.

2. *The Easy Chair:* Sit comfortably in an easy chair, both feet flat on the floor. Let your head rest against the back of the chair, and rest your arms either on the chair arms or on your thighs.

3. *Reclined:* Lie on your back. Have a thin pillow (no more than three inches thick when compressed) under your head, so that the back of your neck can be rested and relaxed. Rest your hands, palms down, at your sides, keeping your elbows slightly bent for comfort. Your feet should be a few inches apart and pointing slightly outward.

The exercise should be done in a quiet place where you will not be disturbed for fifteen minutes.

Instructions

Step One: Put on a Relaxation Mask

Begin with a gentle cycle of deep diaphragmatic breathing.

Now imagine you are putting on an imaginary "relaxation mask." Feel its gentle weight against your skin. All the muscles of your face become relaxed as you put on the mask, smoothing out all frown lines and tension wrinkles. Your eyelids are closed, resting gently, your eyes aimed toward, but not necessarily focusing on, the tip of your nose.

With the imaginary mask in place, the areas above and around your eyes completely relax. Your cheek muscles relax. The muscles around your mouth and jaw relax.

For five minutes, focus on all the feelings of relaxation that having the mask on might induce. Just enjoy these sensations, letting your face fully relax.

Repeat this step of the exercise from two to four times before going on to the next step. If you are following Odessky's recommended plan, do two sessions per day (one in the morning, one in the evening) for two days. You may increase the number of days if you wish.

Hereafter, begin each step with diaphragmatic breathing followed by putting on your imaginary relaxation mask.

Step Two: Create Heaviness

Begin with diaphragmatic breathing. Then put on your relaxation mask.

You will be learning how to create a sensation of heaviness in your dominant arm.

Silently, and purposely, repeat the formula to yourself, as follows:

"My right (or left, if you are left-handed) arm is getting limp and heavy." [Repeat four to six times.]

"My right (left) arm is getting heavier and heavier." [Repeat four to six times.]

"My right (left) arm is completely heavy." [Repeat four to six times.]

"I feel supremely calm and relaxed." [Repeat one time.]

Now open your eyes and get rid of all sensations of heaviness in your arm. Bend your elbow back and forth several times, flicking your wrist gently.

Take three or four diaphragmatic breaths. Check your position and your relaxation mask. Make any adjustments you find necessary.

Begin again, repeating all training phrases exactly as you did the first time. Repetition is vitally important in learning to relax with this program.

Each time you repeat the exercise, imagine your arm getting heavier and heavier, the feeling of relaxation growing more and more distinct.

Do the exercise regularly, but don't try too hard, starting out with clenched teeth and determination and making it a test of your will, since these attitudes will work *against* your intended goal of attaining deep relaxation. Instead, abandon yourself to the repetition formulas and the feeling of heaviness that you will begin to experience almost immediately.

If you have any difficulty imagining the feeling of heaviness, repeat the first exercise in this lesson or hold something heavy in your hand between training sessions. As you get a sense of this heaviness from holding a weighted object, say aloud, "My arm is getting heavier and heavier"; this will help you to associate the real sensations with the phrases in the formula.

Dedication to a training schedule pays off. If you do the exercise at least twice a day for two days you will experience profound sensations of heaviness and relaxation. But take whatever time you wish to get complete results. Your goal is to be thorough, not fast.

After doing the exercise with your dominant arm for two days, use exactly the same formula to repeat the exercise with your nondominant arm. After two days of doing the exercise with your nondominant arm, apply the following formula substitutions, each for two days:

"Both arms are getting limp and heavy."

"My right leg is getting limp and heavy."

"My left leg is getting limp and heavy."

"Both legs are getting limp and heavy."

"My arms and legs are getting limp and heavy."

If you experience genuine feelings of heaviness in *fewer* than the recommended repetitions, go on to the next step of this exercise. But bear in mind that succeeding steps depend upon mastery of the preceding steps.

Step Three: Create Warmth

Here you will learn to create feelings of warmth in your body resulting from blood-flow changes that you will induce.

Begin with diaphragmatic breathing and your imaginary relaxation mask. Continue by performing the complete heaviness exercise for both your arms and legs simultaneously, taking from thirty seconds to one minute. After you have established feelings of heaviness in your arms and legs, begin the exercise for warmth, using the formula below in the same manner as you used the formulas for step one and step two. Begin the warmth exercise *only* after you have established clear feelings of heaviness in step two. If you have any difficulty, repeat the heaviness exercise for the limb you are working on. Warmth will then come more easily.

As you do these exercises for the first time, you may find it helpful to imagine your arms and legs immersed in comfortably warm water. Or you might recall a time at the beach when you were being warmed by the sun. If necessary, put your arm in warm water between sessions, saying to yourself, "My arm is getting warmer and warmer."

> "My right (left, if you are left-handed) arm is getting limp and warm." [Repeat four to six times.]
>
> "My right (left) arm is getting warmer and warmer." [Repeat four to six times.]
>
> "My right (left) arm is completely warm." [Repeat four to six times.]
>
> "I feel supremely calm and warm." [Repeat one time.]

Following the formula, do the exercise with your dominant arm for two days, then with your nondominant arm for two days. Then do both arms. Your right leg. Your left leg. Both legs together. Then both your arms and your legs together simultaneously. Do *each* set for two days.

When you are able to create warmth in both arms, separately and then simultaneously, combine the heaviness and warmth exercises, using the following formula:

"My arms and legs are getting limp, heavy, and warm." [Repeat four to six times.]

"My arms and legs are getting heavier and warmer." [Repeat four to six times.]

"My arms and legs are completely heavy and warm." [Repeat four to six times.]

"I feel supremely calm and relaxed." [Repeat one time.]

Step Four: Calm Your Heart

Now you will learn how to attain a calm, steady heartbeat. Begin this step of the exercise, as with all of the others, with diaphragmatic breathing and the relaxation mask. When you first start working on this step, do the exercise while reclining, since this will allow you to be more conscious of your heart and chest.

Do the entire relaxation process as you have learned it, creating feelings of heaviness and warmth throughout your arms and legs. By now you will be able to create these sensations of relaxation almost instantly.

When you are reclining and relaxed, try to gain a mental sense of your heartbeat. Do this by concentrating either on your chest or on your throat. While relaxed, you will usually get a clear sense of your heartbeat within a few minutes. If you do not, touch your fingers lightly to your pulse on your left wrist, your chest, or on your neck to the left of your windpipe. After you have achieved a sense of your heartbeat, repeat the following formula to yourself:

"My chest feels warm and pleasant." [Repeat four to six times.]

"My heartbeat is calm and steady." [Repeat four to six times.]

"I feel supremely calm and relaxed." [Repeat one time.]

Do this step of the exercise two or three times a day for two weeks, spending seven to ten minutes per session.

Step Five: Create Warmth in Your Stomach

Here you will learn to create a pleasant feeling of warmth in the area between the bottom of your rib cage and your waist.

Begin with diaphragmatic breathing, put on your relaxation mask, and self-induce the feelings of warmth, heaviness, and a calm heart that you have already learned to do. Now add the following (as your skills at creating feelings of relaxation improve, fewer words are needed to induce further relaxation):

> "My stomach is getting warm and soft." [Repeat four to six times.]
> "I feel supremely calm and relaxed." [Repeat one time.]

Do the stomach-warming exercise two times a day for two weeks, spending seven to ten minutes for each session. You will have mastered the exercise when you feel a clear sense of warmth centered in the abdominal area.

If you have difficulty imagining a sense of warmth, rest the palm of your hand on your abdomen above your solar plexus as you do this exercise. Concentrate on the feelings of warmth in the area covered by your hand.

Step Six: Cooling Your Forehead

Here you will learn to create a feeling of coolness on your forehead, a sensation that indicates that excess blood from your head is flowing back to your heart. When this coolness occurs, indicating an actual change in blood flow, deep relaxation follows.

Begin with diaphragmatic breathing, put on your relaxation mask, and then perform the complete relaxation sequence as you have mastered it thus far. Then add:

> "My forehead is cool." [Repeat four to six times.]
> "I feel supremely calm and relaxed." [Repeat one time.]

As you say the words to yourself, imagine a fresh breeze as it gently cools your forehead. Should you need to create the actual sensation, stand in front of a fan or air conditioner, set at low speed, and say aloud, "My forehead is cool."

You will have completed this lesson when you have succeeded in creating the sensation of coolness on your forehead as well as the sensations of warmth in your abdomen and heaviness and warmth in your limbs.

Putting It All Together

Having mastered all six steps of Phase Three, you now need a formula for putting it all together. The following is a short reference list for perfecting a smooth and rhythmic relaxation routine. By memorizing it you will always have all the instructions you will ever need with you:

Deep diaphragmatic breathing—three breaths.

My relaxation mask is on.

My face feels smooth and relaxed.

My arms and legs are limp, heavy, and warm.

My arms and legs are getting heavier and warmer.

My arms and legs are completely heavy and warm.

My heartbeat is calm and steady.

I feel supremely calm and relaxed.

My stomach feels soft and warm.

I feel supremely calm and relaxed.

My forehead feels cool.

I feel supremely calm and relaxed.

As you gain mastery of this exercise, you will find that you can induce a deeply relaxed state by simply sitting down, taking three diaphragmatic breaths, and thinking to yourself: "Mask in place. Facial muscles smooth. Arms and legs heavy and warm. Heart calm and steady. Stomach warm. Forehead cool. Supremely calm and relaxed."

End each session gradually and calmly. Open your eyes gently. Move around very slowly at first. Stretch yourself, and throw off your sense of heaviness, warmth, and relaxation. Lightly run in place, shake your hands, and so on. Be physically active, and the benefits of relaxation will begin to appear in the form of increased alertness, increased energy, and an improved ability to concentrate on whatever activity you choose to do.

SUMMARY

After successfully completing all three phases of Lesson Three, you will possess a new range of skills that will allow you to:

Create a state of mind-body integration that sports psychologists show is conducive to optimal performance, and that is achieved by relaxing for ten to fifteen minutes at least twenty to thirty minutes before competition.

Monitor the sensations of tension and relaxation that you might experience before or during a game. Using knowledge gained in Phase One, you can identify muscle groups throughout your body that require greater relaxation. The degree of relaxation desired in specific muscles can then be achieved either through diaphragmatic breathing or through autogenic training.

Use diaphragmatic breathing (which you learned in Phase Two) to place your mind and body in a state of alert and relaxed readiness prior to competition.

Enjoy in only fifteen or twenty minutes refreshing benefits similar to those derived from much longer periods of sleep. This skill is especially valuable in resting yourself just prior to a game when you have not gotten a good night's sleep, in aiding recuperation between playing periods of a game, and in speeding recuperation after a strenuous game or workout.

Coordinate the physical and mental capabilities of the right and left hemispheres of the brain, facilitating cerebral activity back and forth between the two. This allows you to control a too-active left brain so that the right brain, with its visualizing skills, can also play the game. This is a Phase Three skill.

Establish increased emotional control to better handle moments of frustration, fear, anger, or anxiety. Although athletic poise will not be presented until Lesson Five, your work in relaxation and breathing techniques will enable you to begin reaping benefits immediately. Most athletes realize an increase in emotional control almost immediately upon completion of Lesson 3.

In the next lesson, on mental rehearsal, building from what you have just learned about relaxation, you will learn how to create mental imagery that will guide your mind and body for optimal performance in your sport.

APPLICATIONS FOR THIS LESSON OUTSIDE SPORTS

Career/Business: The same relaxation skills you have learned in Lesson 3 are being taught in stress reduction programs for business people throughout the country. The research showing the effects of stress on muscular coordination and mental readiness in sports applies to business in only a slightly different way. Whereas the pressure of competition in the sports arena may be manifest in the body as a loss of precise control in physical movements, pressure in business or in a profession can be manifest in the body as so-called stress diseases: ulcers, digestive problems, susceptibility to infections (especially upper respiratory diseases), backaches, and heart disease. Some authorities say even cancer may have a stress component.

Mental faculties are also affected by stress. Whereas the pressure of competition for the athlete can result in poor judgments on the playing field, it can result in diminished productivity, lack of energy to make important decisions, lack of motivation, and a reluctance to communicate adequately to co-workers.

By developing the ability to relax at will, as I have described to you in this lesson, you have at your disposal a set of the most powerful mental skills ever invented for combating stress. Peak performers in industry develop these relaxation skills and practice them prior to important meetings in the same way that professional athletes practice them prior to going onto the playing field.

To many executives with whom I've worked, the idea of relaxing prior to negotiating a difficult contract seems contradictory. But when they learn how relaxation frees them of the stereotypical responses of fight or flight, this sense of contradiction disappears. You have only to remember that the relaxation skills learned in this lesson release hidden reserves that increase mental alertness, prevent irrational responses to the most frustrating hurdles, and keep you mentally tracked on your most positive long-term goal.

Personal: For nearly two decades now, medical professionals have been demonstrating the importance of the relaxation response in building personal health. My coauthor Hal Zina Bennett, along with Dr. Mike Samuels *(The Well Body Book),* has been in the forefront of the *wellness* or *self-help health movement,* through which we have seen developed effective techniques for fully utilizing the health-building aspects of relaxation. The work of Harvard physician Herbert Benson (author of *The Relaxation Response)* and Norman Cousins (former *Saturday Review* editor, UCLA faculty member, and author of *The Healing Heart)* have been particularly helpful to large numbers of readers.

Through the pressures of modern life and psychological habit, we impose chronic tension on our bodies. Sometimes this is a localized tension, such as in the muscles of the neck, shoulders, and chest, resulting in tension headaches, aching muscles, susceptibility to colds, flu, and other respiratory infections, and even heart and respiratory complaints or diseases. Sometimes the tension is systemic, affecting virtually every cell in the body. Basically, the relaxation response allows the body to *normalize*. This means that vital functions, such as the circulation of blood and lymph, the heart and respiration, hormonal responses, and self-healing mechanisms, (that is, immunity and tissue rebuilding), are allowed to find their own optimal levels, thus delivering maximum health benefits to the entire organism.

The kind of tension you manifest in your body can be identified through Phase One, Exploring Relaxation and Tension, of this lesson. You can then follow this up by learning Phase Two, Breathing for Peak Performance, and then Phase Three, Autogenic Training.

Schendel, Cynthia

MENTAL REHEARSAL

Using the Powers of the Mind
to Perfect Your Performance

I never hit a shot, not even in practice, without having a very sharp, in-focus picture of it in my head.

Jack Nicklaus
golfer

In this lesson you will learn mental rehearsal techniques using your imagination to create mental images of yourself performing at optimal levels. This technique is the single most powerful tool in the Soviet mental training arsenal. It enables you to build confidence, accelerate reaction times, and improve physical coordination and accuracy, and it allows you to work out complex strategies before executing them.

THE POWER OF DISCIPLINED IMAGINATION

Mental rehearsal is by no means unknown to most athletes. But the formalization of the technique and its systematic use in athletic training programs, as has been done in the Soviet Union, is quite new to us. And whereas the Russians and East Germans use the technique in routine "mental workouts" as a way to maximize performance capabilities, mental rehearsal has been applied in the United States largely to correct, rather than to prevent, problems. The Soviet psychologist Gregory Raiport, who worked with Russian national teams from 1972 to 1976, has commented that the Russian and American applications of mental training seem at times to be at opposite poles—the former directed to the creation of athletic excellence, the latter to the correction of chronic deficiencies.

What exactly is mental rehearsal? Raiport has explained how mental rehearsal is used to help train athletes at the National Research Institute of Physical Culture in Moscow: in their mental rehearsal sessions, the Russian athletes are taught to "imagine or visualize themselves performing the different stages of the event," and by doing so they actually supplement their physical training by providing themselves with invaluable neuromuscular practice.

According to Raiport, the purpose of mental training is to achieve "that special state of facility when everything happens precisely and, it seems, effortlessly." Through mental rehearsal, athletes are able to achieve levels of performance only briefly experienced in their athletic careers. Building on their brief experiences of success, Soviet athletes are taught to mentally create *neuromuscular templates,* that is, examples of the ideal ways to move, preparing them eventually to manifest those *inner* rehearsals in *external* actions. The mechanism for this is one of the most commonly acknowledged in human psychology. Called "modeling," it is the same process children go through as they find examples for their own behavior in the behavior of the people around them. Mental rehearsal, according to Raiport, is the creative and disciplined use of the imagination, the object of which is to "perfect athletic movement."

During mental rehearsal, neuromuscular processes are put through their paces. These processes are the invisible workings of the brain making connections with the muscles, and the muscles signaling back to the brain—a constant biofeedback loop without which there could be no movement of any kind. Much of the current work in this area draws from the research of Nobel scientist Roger Sperry. When I first heard about mental rehearsal, I was reminded of the Apollo project, where the men and women assigned to Mission Control rehearsed the roles they would play in guiding the LEM spacecraft to the moon and back. They practiced their roles as elements of a gigantic and vital technological mind for months before the spaceship was finally launched. I also learned that our astronauts were logging many hours in spaceflight simulators, training their reflexes for an event that no human had ever experienced. Imagination provided the mental images for rehearsing a complex network of events that was to take place in the future.

The disciplined use of the imagination for improving sports performance is without a doubt one of the chief contributions the Soviets have made to the art and science of mental training. During his visit to the Soviet Union in 1978, James Hickman interviewed a number of Soviet sports psychologists and questioned them about athletic training programs in both Russia and East Germany. He concluded, "Imagination is probably the most widely applied mental process in modern sports." In comparing training programs East and West, Hickman said, "Learning to influence your physiology mentally is an important missing ingredient in most Western training systems," and he said that the disciplined use of the imagination as pioneered by the Soviets "can carry us into territories of performance and ability far beyond what most of us generally imagine."

RULES OF MOTION IN MENTAL REHEARSAL

An important requirement of practicing mental rehearsal is that the mental images *must include movement.*

In his study on the effects of mental rehearsal on fifty-three alpine skiers, Swedish sports psychologist Lars-Eric Unestahl found that the most positive results were obtained when athletes created mental images of *actions* rather than of static postures. The temptation for many people just starting out with mental rehearsal is to create "still shots" of positions that they know, in principle, are correct. This has the effect of *freezing* the mental image, a little like what happens when film gets stuck in a motion-picture projector. But because motion is the essence of sports, movement and one's response to the changing circumstances created by movement *must* be included in the rehearsal. Thus, Unestahl instructed his athletes: "Tell your body what to do by thinking through the run—that is, imaging yourself skiing down. Then start your body and let it do the rest. The task while you are skiing down will be to sing, hum, or whistle a melody."

According to Unestahl, the highest number of negative results was produced when athletes created mental images that focused on specific postures, and in so doing subconsciously directed their bodies to remain set in particular positions—even when they were performing complex actions that required constant change in response to changing circumstances. The following is the example Unestahl presents of a mental rehearsal that has *negative* effects on performance: "Concentrate on the following things while you are skiing down: a) arms forward, easily bent, the underarms parallel to the ground; b) initiate the turn: sink down and put your poles down during the raising up; c) the vertical work: turn the skis when you are in the highest position; d) the turn: bring your hip in toward the hill and compensate with your upper body down while sinking down."

Unestahl's point is subtle, but if you imagine how you would feel if you were to ski down a hill while trying to remember this long list of static instructions, you will probably clutch up just thinking about it.

In Unestahl's recommendations for positive results, the athletes create *moving mental images* that allow them to respond fully to the changes and movement necessary to the execution of the actions they are preparing to perform. It has been my experience in working with athletes that movement in the imagery prepares the body and mind for change, ultimately allowing the athletes to respond to the present even as they are being guided by mental imagery. With movement and change programmed into the mental image, they can then let the mind and body take over. Once the action actually begins, the athletes turn their attention away from *deliberate mental activity* by whistling or humming. Conscious, deliberate thought ceases, and the images of action take over automatically.

The mental images that athletes create are what Stanford University researcher Karl Pribram has called *mental holograms,* three-dimensional mental images that direct nerve impulses to all the muscles of the body that will be involved in the actual execution of a task. As long as we allow these holograms to direct our movements—and the word *movement* is the key here—those moves in real life will be smooth, confident, and precise. When we try to give our bodies more direct, verbal (left brain) orders—with images becoming static, as in the negative example presented earlier—our movements become choppy, we lose confidence, and we make mistakes.

A number of sports scientists have shown that when mental rehearsal, which includes movements, is practiced by conditioned athletes, *it is as effective and beneficial as the actual physical training they do for their sports.* For example, sports psychologist Lee Pulos of the University of British Columbia worked with the Canadian National Women's Volleyball Team, having them practice various movements through mental rather than physical rehearsal. He told one player to imagine a particular shot she would be making. She visualized this movement hundreds of times, until she had vivid images of it in her mind. With the mental rehearsal well established, she began to practice the shot on the court. There on the court, mental rehearsal and physical activity became one. The result was a nearly flawless execution of movement.

Pulos has said, "What [athletes] have ideally executed in their minds' eyes, they will be able to translate into action during practice or competition." He also said that by creating the ideal imagery, the athlete is "laying the proper neurological tracks" for optimal performance, overriding previously laid, faulty tracks.

In 1978, sports psychologist Barbara Kolonay tested basketball players using mental rehearsal during free-throw shooting at New York's Hunter College. With eight teams, two of which were used as control groups, individual improvement in the performance of players using mental rehearsal was as high as 15 percent. The process began with a relaxation segment similar to the one presented in Lesson 3, followed by a mental rehearsal segment. In the latter, each athlete sat in a straight-backed chair and, when in a deeply relaxed state, was asked to imagine going through the entire process of standing on the free-throw line, being handed the ball, hearing the crowd, making the shot, and then seeing the ball go through the hoop.

Hunter College psychologists reviewing Kolonay's reports concluded, "Imagery builds confidence." In addition, when electromyograms were taken of Kolonay's subjects during the mental rehearsal segment, it was found that their "muscles actually performed the exact motions imagined," putting the players through their paces on a subliminal level.

In research with athletes in the Soviet Union, Alexander Romen showed that athletes' reaction times could be accelerated through the use of the mental rehearsal technique. In reviewing Romen's work on mental rehearsal and self-regulation training, Stanley Krippner said that there could be no doubt that these techniques were invaluable in "improving and enhancing just about any human function or ability desired."

MENTAL REHEARSAL: A LONG BUT QUIET TRADITION IN THE WEST

All peak performers I have interviewed report that they use some form of mental rehearsal in both training and competition. However, most have come upon this skill by either chance or trial and error rather than through formal training. Commenting on the lack of mental training in the United States, Gregory Raiport has said that, "A first-grader in the Soviet Union gets more help than Olympic-caliber athletes do here." It is useful for us to see how many of our own athletes do use mental rehearsal, not only so that we may understand *how* they do this but also in order to learn the extent to which they feel it improves their performance.

One of the most articulate athletes on the subject of mental rehearsal is golfer Jack Nicklaus, who calls his use of this technique "going to the movies." He imagines each shot in his mind before he executes it.

Tennis champion Chris Evert-Lloyd once said in a radio interview that before every game she painstakingly rehearses every significant detail of a match in her mind.

Bill Russell, of basketball fame, has described his use of mental rehearsal in great detail: "I was sitting there with my eyes closed, watching plays in my head. . . . It was effortless; the movies I saw in my head seemed to have their own projector, and whenever I closed my eyes it would run. . . . With only a little mental discipline I could keep myself focused on plays I had actually seen, and so many of them were new that I never felt bored."

Do *all* athletes create mental images of their plays prior to the game? In a number of research reports, the Soviets have demonstrated that they do—and these mental images can sometimes be a problem. According to the Soviets' National Institute of Physical Culture, negative as well as positive imagery shapes the athlete's actions. Anxiety, low self-esteem, fear of failure, and old habits can all become part of the mental images the athlete carries into actual play. This can result in diversion of attention from the game and can also create muscular tension that can destroy or impair physical performance. We overcome or eliminate faulty visualization when we create, and repeatedly practice, visualizations of the *proper* execution of a movement. Proper mental rehearsal is really nothing more than learning to use your mental capacities in a positive way, effectively *choosing,* rather than leaving to chance, the neurological patterns that will guide your movements.

PRACTICING STRATEGIES BEFORE THE GAME

We are all familiar with the reverse of mental rehearsal—reviewing mistakes after the fact. Hours after a heated confrontation, we think of all the things we *should have said.* In sports in which strategy is employed, as in most team sports, a similar mechanism is often applied, but *in advance*. For example, Fran Tarkenton, whose passing record ranks among the best in the National Football League, described how he visualized a game days before it took place, speaking of himself in the third person:

> This week, he must think "Pittsburgh," and nothing else. He must see that Steeler defense in his dreams, every one of them, knowing their names, numbers, bodies, moves. He must be able to know who is chasing him by the sound of the footsteps, and which way to turn to evade him, for every man has his weakness. He must see those linebackers eyeing him as they backtrack into pass coverage, know their relative speeds and effectiveness, know just how many steps each one will take on specific defensive calls so that he can find the right hole at the right time.

It is interesting to note how Tarkenton created his visual images from sensory data, *seeing* every one of his opponents, knowing the *sound* of their footsteps, visualizing gaps in the offensive line so that he could "find the right hole at the right time." All of these are examples of right brain dominance, from which the mental holograms are made that direct our physical actions.

Tarkenton described how he visualized all the possible plays in an upcoming game, rehearsing the future in his mind, the way a choreographer might rehearse a large dance troupe on the stage: "By Friday, I'm running whole blocks of plays in my head. . . . I'm trying to visualize every game situation, every defense they're going to throw at me. I tell myself, 'What will I do on their five-yard line and it's third and goal to go, and our short passing game hasn't been going too well, and their line looks like a wall, and we're six points behind?'"

Bill Russell had still another way of using his visual imaging powers, and although his is an intricate process, it provides a model for an immensely useful mental tool that anyone can adopt. Russell talks about watching other players, holding his images of their best moves in his mind, and then allowing those images to become the pictures that will direct his actions.

He used this technique not only for developing new moves but also for correcting moves that didn't work: "If I had a play in my mind but muffed it on the court, I'd go over it repeatedly in my head, searching for details I'd missed. I'd goofed because I'd overlooked a critical detail in my mind, so I'd go back to check my model." By comparing what he saw and did on the court with the images he carried in his mind, Russell was able to make adjustments and corrections in his own behavior that would later result in improved performance. "I'd think of a move and run it through my mind. Then I'd try it—once, twice, three times. Usually I'd make adjustments after each try, but occasionally I'd get it right the first go."

Russell also tells how he used his "movies" for developing his own defensive skills, something that happened more by chance than design, according to him. Watching another player, he would "take a film" with his mental camera, and would later run this in his mind, putting himself opposite that player: "I'd imagine myself as his mirror image; I'd take a step backward for every step he took forward, and so forth. It was as if we were dancing."

The reflexes Russell developed through this method contributed to his enormous success as a defensive player. Reflecting on his first indication that this was happening, he says: "I was happy because those defensive moves were the first that I'd invented on my own and then made real. I didn't copy them; I invented them. They grew out of my imagination."

Michael Murphy, cofounder of the Esalen Institute and a researcher on the bodily changes that sometimes accompany states of altered consciousness in sports, speaks of how mental imagery can bring about dramatic physiological changes:

> Muscles may be recontoured, fat may disappear, new capillaries—thousands of miles of them—may develop, organelles may be added to cells, tendons may be stretched and made more flexible. This happens naturally, of course, through the physical exercise the athlete does. Each sport or training regimen determines what the athlete's body will be like. But the process can be aided by suggestion, visualization, and other mental techniques.

My firsthand experience as a power lifter and bodybuilder leaves little doubt in my mind that Murphy's observations are correct. I have heard both Arnold Schwarzenegger and Frank Zane, both multiple Mr. Olympia winners, speak of how they have used visualization to sculpt their bodies. Of his use of mental rehearsal and visualization, Schwarzenegger said, "A pump when I see the muscle I want is worth ten with my mind drifting."

MENTAL REHEARSAL AND TIME ALTERATION

A number of peak performers I have studied speak of the experience of "time alteration," when the inner clocks that regulate their senses of time radically change during the performance of an activity. Italian diver Klaus DiBiasi, the only person in history to win three successive Olympic gold medals in platform diving, described how "in competition, the seconds that you are in the air seem very long. . . . [It] feels as if it is taking you one minute for the dive instead of only a few seconds."

For any activity in which precise performance of complex movements must occur in a short period of time, it is necessary to mentally rehearse many movements in great detail. The rehearsal itself appears to account for the sense that time is being altered. DiBiasi explained that after mentally rehearsing every movement in the dive, there is the illusion of time being altered "because you pay attention to the dive and you can remember each small amount of that dive." What happens, apparently, is that the mental rehearsal *elongates* the action, spreading out into a few minutes all the movements the athlete must execute in a second in competition. Then, in competition, the reverse happens—the mind flashes back to the rehearsal and creates an illusion that there is all the time in the world to execute the action.

Race drivers, who, like divers, must perform complex operations at high speeds, report a similar slowing of time. In an interview, Jackie Stewart vividly recalled the experience of going into a turn at speeds approaching 200 miles per hour: "At 195 miles per hour, you should still have a very clear vision, almost in slow motion, of going through that corner, so that you have time to brake, time to line the car up, and time to recognize the amount of drift—and then you've hit the apex, given it a bit of a tweak, hit the exit, and are out at 173 miles per hour."

Stewart commented that the driver "who doesn't have a mental picture in advance will arrive at the corner to find that it's all happening too quickly." He concluded that the driver who fails to master mental rehearsal "doesn't have it" to succeed in this sport.

Some of the most dramatic examples of the alteration of time sense have been associated with team sports, where decisions must be made quickly, under great pressure, and often in the face of much confusion. In an interview with Mike Murphy in *Intellectual Digest,* John Brodie said that there are moments in every game when "time seems to slow way down, in an uncanny way, as if everyone were moving in slow motion. . . . It seems as if I had all the time in the world to watch the receivers run their patterns, and yet I know the defensive line is coming at me just as fast as ever."

Time alteration, which releases the athlete from the pressure of time, occurs naturally with mental rehearsal. But to accomplish it, it is necessary to rehearse *each increment of movement,* especially for those activities that occur very quickly in real time. For example, if you're a diver, rehearse each increment of movement from the beginning to the end of the dive, so that mental rehearsal seems to be a slow-motion replay of a videotape. Then, in actual competition, it seems as though the inner clock is slowed down, providing a sense of having all the time in the world to do what has to be done.

CONCENTRATION AND MENTAL REHEARSAL

Mental rehearsal increases concentration through deep relaxation, which erases thoughts and feelings from the mind and body. Once this is achieved, the mind can be compared to a blank screen upon which we project the moving images that will direct our athletic actions.

During mental rehearsal, you prepare the inner world (your mind) to match the outer world (the athletic event). Concentration increases because we are internally prepared to relate *only* to that which contributes something of substance to the anticipated performance.

Remembering that the Soviets spent years studying Zen and the martial arts, we know that we're on the right track when we turn to the martial artists for confirmation of our view of mental rehearsal and concentration. Joe Hyams wrote in his book *Zen in the Martial Arts,* about his lessons with Master Bong Soo Han, a Korean hapkido expert. Hyams quoted Master Han: "As long as what you are doing at the moment is *exactly* what you are doing at that moment and nothing else, you are one with yourself and with what you are doing—and that is Zen; while doing something, you are doing it at the fullest."

In the state that Master Han described, you can expect quicker reaction times because superfluous signals to the muscles are minimized. Confidence increases because you avoid dwelling on the past, where you could find experiences of failure upon which to dwell. Fears are reduced and confidence further enhanced when you maintain both inner and outer focus in the present time rather than letting your imagination drift into the future, where the *possibilities* for failure, or even physical injury, are unlimited.

When the mental rehearsal is synchronous with the event in which you are engaged, you enter what many athletes refer to as a "cocoon of concentration." When that level of concentration is achieved, you experience what Lars-Eric Unestahl has called the "winning feeling," a feeling that you and the action you are performing are all that exist in the world. In the final anlaysis, the cocoon of concentration is an extraordinary experience that not only releases massive reserves of energy that are ordinarily not available but also provides an experience unlike anything else.

We have discussed how images of athletic movement created in the mind prepare neuromuscular mechanisms for optimal performance. A number of research projects have demonstrated significant improvement in the performance records of athletes who employ mental rehearsal in sports in which they already possess a degree of proficiency.

Western athletes have a tradition of using mental rehearsal for working out plays, perfecting difficult movements, inventing new plays, and sculpting muscles. Finally, we explored how time alteration is related to mental rehearsal and how this technique allows you to execute athletic sequences requiring complex and precise movements in short spans of time.

Remember that all mental rehearsal, regardless of the sport, depends on certain key skills. In the exercises that follow, you will learn how to develop these skills.

SEEING WITH YOUR MIND'S EYE Phase One

Time: One 15-to-20-minute session

Benefits: This exercise serves as a preliminary for the more complex mental rehearsal exercises to follow. Through the learning of proper visual imagery and rehearsal techniques, confusion is dispelled and accuracy is improved.

In the instructions for mental rehearsal, you will be asked to create mental images that correspond to the movements or tasks you want to accomplish in your sport. Some people have difficulty and become frustrated when they feel unable to produce what they believe is meant by "mental imagery." It is important to realize that not everyone produces images that are as clear as those on a TV screen.

Over the years, I have conducted a number of informal experiments to determine what people actually do see when they are asked to visualize an event from the past. One woman, a swimmer, said that she could remember, but could not create a mental image of, a friend with whom she had learned to swim as a child. I asked her to recall this friend as best she could, to access her memory of the two of them swimming. After a few moments, the woman told me that she had the memory clearly in her mind, and that what she felt was reliving that experience. I asked her to tell me what this person was wearing and saying and to note some object in the environment in which the activity was taking place. Although she claimed to have no clear image in her mind, she gave me clear visual descriptions of everything I requested. I was convinced by this and by similar experiments that *everyone* is able to create effective mental imagery, even though not everyone recognizes it as such while creating it.

Everyone creates mental images in his or her own distinct way. To discover exactly how *you* do this, you may want to recall a close friend or a relative, an athletic event in which you participated, a special place you visited on a vacation, or even an object that has special meaning for you. As a warm-up prior to this exercise, recall the person, event, or object as vividly as you can.

Give yourself a few moments to become comfortable and familiar with this memory.

Now explore what it is that you are "seeing." Is there an actual image in your mind, similar to what you would see when looking at a photograph or watching television? If you don't *see* something in your mind, do you have a clear visual *impression,* as though what you are recalling is really quite clear to you? Can you identify certain colors? Can you identify or describe a shape or a texture that you know is there in your mind's eye, even though you cannot, in the ordinary sense, *see* them?

If you have clear visual images in your mind, similar to what you would see in a photograph or in real life, then that is your particular way of visualizing. On the other hand, if you have only *impressions* of a person, event, or object—impressions that nevertheless feel real to you and project you back in time—then *that* is your individual way of visualizing.

But what about even more auditory or abstract impressions? A diffuse impression may be anything from the recollection of a sensation (qualities of light, sounds, scents, tastes, touch, bodily feelings, and so on) to the recollection of certain emotions such as exaltation or anger associated with the image. These are all valid visualizations, and they will serve you effectively in mental rehearsal.

To some, mental imagery consists of muscular sensations, or what I call the *inner experience* of movement. This type of mental imagery is frequently reported by elite athletes.

Your mental rehearsal may consist of any or all of these elements. The exact way in which you create your mental image or impression is not as important as your feeling that it is vividly sketched in your mind's eye. The following exercise will help you develop skills in voluntarily creating these mental images at will.

Preparation
Do the exercise when you will not be disturbed for fifteen to twenty minutes. Begin by achieving a deeply relaxed state, as you learned to do in Lesson 3.

Instructions
Recall a person, event, or object that is particularly meaningful to you. As you bring this image to your mind, explore it in detail. See how many fine points you can recall—colors, textures, sounds, emotions, smells, and so on.

> *Example:* I recall the 1973 Camaro convertible I bought just after my college graduation. It is a metallic gold color. It has spoked wheels and wide tires with white sidewalls. The body has smooth, flowing lines. I open the door, climb into the comfortable leather driver's seat and take the wheel. As I grip the wheel, I am aware of the texture of the leather steering wheel cover and how it feels against my skin. For a moment I study the dashboard, the neat, businesslike layout of the instrument panel. I reach out, switch on the ignition, depress the accelerator and listen to the confident rumble of the engine. I push in the clutch, slide the gearshift lever into first, and ease forward. In a moment I'm racing down the highway at fifty-five miles an hour. The top is down. It's a warm day. I feel the wind in my hair.

Example: Perry and I are running down Evergreen Street as we usually do in the evenings after work. It is a warm evening, and we're both feeling good. We talk about nothing in particular as we run, though the talking seems to create a sense of camaraderie between us.

Allow yourself a few moments to visualize your mental image and explore it at your own pace.

Now take a deep breath, hold it for a count of four, and exhale slowly. As you do, you may notice that your mental image becomes clearer in detail. As you relax, blood flow increases, energizing the brain's visual cortex, where mental imagery occurs. If clarity does not occur immediately, stimulate your visual cortex further by taking another deep breath and recalling additional visual details. If your mental image is a person, a detail might be a particular facial expression. If your mental image is an object, recall a color or texture of a particular area. Focus your attention on as many other details as possible.

Now erase this image from your mind. Do this by looking toward an artifical light *with your eyes closed.* Create in your mind a sense of neutral space with the help of the light. The color you see should be neutral: beige, gray, or pale pink. Some people create a mental image of neutral space with no apparent boundaries or color. Others create a blank mental visual field, not unlike a television or movie screen having no picture.

For a moment, focus only on this neutral space.

After approximately twenty seconds, recall the mental image of the person, event, or object you previously created. If you perceive an image other than the one you first created, erase the image, return to visualizing the neutral space, and start again.

As simple as this exercise may seem, not everyone will be able to master it immediately. Be persistent and systematic in your practice. If necessary, repeat the exercise daily for several days until you can create a vivid image, then erase it, create a neutral space, and then re-create the original image. The degree of control you develop over mental imagery will determine your ultimate success at using mental rehearsal.

YOUR BEST PERFORMANCE AND BEYOND
Phase Two

Time: Three 20-minute sessions

Benefits: You will learn how to create mental images that serve as a model for future peak performance, based on past performances or on segments of past performances done extremely well.

In this exercise, you will recall your best past performance in the athletic event you want to develop.

The best performance can be one segment of a larger event, such as one particular serve in a game of tennis, one putt in eighteen holes of golf, a ten-minute segment in an hour-long run, and so on.

If your best performance happens to be one in which you won a competition, by all means use it. However, the significant event is a period of time that, *regardless of the competitive outcome,* provided an experience of actualization that corresponds to the peak performance experience described in Lesson 1. In other words, mentally scan your personal history for moments of high volitional preference and mind-body integration. You may want to review the volition clusters you prepared in Lesson 1 to solidly recall such moments.

For example, if your best performance was in playing basketball and sinking the free throw that ultimately resulted in victory for your team, recall the entire experience vividly. Relive, in your mind's eye, everything about the experience. Imagine yourself standing on the free-throw line. You hear the squeak of shoes on the court as players line up. You hear the crowd and feel the excitement as the ball is handed to you. You hold the ball for a moment, feeling its texture, its perfect roundness, perhaps its smell. You bounce it, letting it return to your hands. You feel very good inside, completely in control of yourself, confident in your ability. You take the ball in both hands, line up and focus your attention on the rim. You concentrate, shoot. You watch the ball rise through its arc, fall, drop through the center of the rim, swish effortlessly through the net.

When you create your mental images, keep in mind that the timing of the images you create should be as close as you can make it to the duration of the actual event. It might even be helpful to use a stopwatch, first timing an actual event and then patterning the mental rehearsal accordingly. Note here that when mentally rehearsing actions that take place very quickly, such as in diving or in steering through a series of high-speed curves in auto racing, your initial rehearsals may elongate time. However, once you have mentally rehearsed the actions through this elongation process you should be able to mentally rehearse the action in the time period required in actual performance.

Synchronizing mental rehearsal timing with real performance timing is particularly important in sports such as downhill skiing where the entire event takes place in a brief period of time.

Richard Suinn, of the department of psychology at Colorado State University, measured responses of an alpine ski racer by electromyographs as the skier recalled moment-by-moment imagery of a race. Suinn reported:

> Almost instantly, the recording needles stirred into action. Two muscle bursts appeared as the skier hit jumps. Additional muscle bursts duplicated the effort of crossing a rough section of the course, and the needles settled during the easy sections. By the time he finished this psychological rehearsal of the downhill race, his EMG recordings almost mirrored the course itself. There was even a final burst of muscle activity after he had passed the finish line, a mystery to me until I remembered how hard it is to come to a skidding stop after racing downhill at more than forty miles an hour.

It is equally important to rehearse mentally the *complete* action, rather than just the beginning, middle, end, or any other segment. Jack Nicklaus makes a point of telling golfers that "visualizing the swing is useless if you fail to visualize what it's supposed to achieve." In his book, *Golf My Way*, Nicklaus described exactly how he puts this principle into action: "First I 'see' the ball where I want it to finish, nice and white and sitting up high on the bright green grass. Then the scene quickly changes, and I 'see' the ball going there: its path, trajectory, and shape, even its behavior on landing. Then there is sort of a fade-out, and the next scene shows me making the kind of swing that will turn the previous images into reality."

Obviously, not every athletic event can be visualized in its entirety. For example, you can not visualize an entire football or basketball game. Therefore, mentally rehearse the key segments, particularly those in which your role is a primary factor.

The number of times you were able to repeat your best performance in real life is insignificant in choosing an experience for mental rehearsal. It is, however, important to focus your mental energy on this event, creating a vivid picture of it in your mind's eye, remembering that it will soon become a mental blueprint that will affect further performances.

Rehearse creating mental imagery of your best performance again and again, in your home or in the locker room, until you can easily recall it in its entirety, whenever you wish. When you can create a clear practice at will, take the rehearsal to the field. Five to ten minutes prior to performing the actual activity, recall your mental rehearsal technique. Relive every detail, feeling it in your body as you do. Relax as you recall the mental images.

Preparation

Review your volition clusters charts from Lesson 1. In some cases, it will be helpful to make certain that the performance level you are attempting has a high probability of success; if you have doubts, review the goals chart you prepared in

Lesson 2. The following exercise should be done at a time when you will not be disturbed for at least twenty minutes. Your ability to complete this mental rehearsal exercise quickly and with ease is a prerequisite to employing this technique in actual performance.

Instructions

Step One: Relax

To create complete and vivid mental images, achieve deep relaxation, which you learned in Lesson 3, prior to starting the visualizing activity.

Step Two: Know the Performance You Will Recall

Before you begin, be certain that the performance you have chosen is attainable within the limits of this exercise. For example, if you are a tennis player, you will want to recall a specific serve in your best performance, rather than recalling an entire set. Mental rehearsal of the serve can be easily employed in practice alone or before an actual game. If you are a runner, you might want to rehearse mentally a single lap around the track or a run along a particular segment of a course, rather than trying to visualize an hour-long run. It may take some experimentation before you know exactly what you need to visualize. The best test of a visualization is that after mentally rehearsing the activity three or four times you should be able to run through it effortlessly.

Step Three: The Visualization

While in a deeply relaxed state, either sitting or lying down, close your eyes and recall that moment of your best performance or the best segment of a performance that you have chosen for this exercise.

Focus on the part of your body that was most intensely involved in performing this activity. Were your feet or legs most involved? Your arms? Or was your entire body involved?

How did your leg muscles feel? Try to feel these sensations

in your legs again. How did your buttocks and back feel? Relive these sensations. Your arms? Your neck and shoulders? Your chest? Abdomen? Pelvis? Let yourself vividly recall whatever bodily sensations come to mind.

What thoughts and feelings did you have as you were performing? Did you feel relaxed? Were you proud of what you were accomplishing?

Who, if anyone, was with you, either as a fellow participant in the activity or as a spectator? Recall any details that come to mind about the person or persons: things you talked about, a facial expression, perhaps what they were wearing or how they moved.

What did you see? You may find that you now recall an important visual clue: the way the ground moved toward you as you ran, the speed at which you passed objects beside you, the way a ball moved away from you as you threw it, or the way it moved as someone threw it to you. Pay particular attention to the way a ball made contact with a racket, bat, or other piece of equipment you might have used.

If a ball is involved in your sport, visualize exactly what you want it to do as you complete whatever action you are rehearsing. The football reaches the outstretched hands of the receiver. The served tennis ball should hit exactly the right spot on the court. The basketball swishes through the net. The golf ball drops into the cup, and so on.

Recall sounds: The distinct sound of the tennis ball when you served it. The crack of the bat. The sound of your footsteps or your breathing as you ran. The whirring sound of spokes or the dull, almost ringing sounds of the chain on your bicycle as you rode. The heavy metallic ring of the weights as you made a successful power lift.

Create pictures, sounds, and sensations of all kinds to join in your mental rehearsal, enriching it. Often the embellishments come automatically, similar to free association in a verbal process, and you do not need to do anything deliberate to bring them forth. Furthermore, such recollections are automatically integrated into your visualization.

Step Four: Assign Trigger Words

When you have rehearsed to the point where visualization of the event seems to come to life effortlessly (usually after three times), choose one word that accurately describes or names the event. This will be the *trigger word.* You will use the trigger word to elicit a replay of what you have mentally rehearsed whenever you wish to make use of it. Even though the number of sensations constituting the visualization may seem extensive, they all combine to form a complete visual image that will come alive, whenever you wish, through the use of a single trigger word. This word should describe or name the action you are rehearsing: for example, *serve, hit, score, spin,* and so on.

In the initial stages, repeat the trigger word to yourself at the beginning and the end of each mental rehearsal. After a few times, the word and the rehearsal will be so strongly reinforced or conditioned that the mere suggestion of the word will elicit replay of the rehearsed mental imagery, just as Pavlov's dogs would ultimately salivate upon the mere ringing of a bell.

Step Five: From Rehearsal to Action

Whenever you are doing warm-ups, take time either before or after to relax and visualize, using the mental rehearsal technique that you have learned. Relaxation and rehearsal need not take long. As your mental skills develop, you will find that you will need to close your eyes for only a moment and replay only once the mental images you have refined through rehearsal.

When long and varied actions are a part of a game, you will want to use mental rehearsal techniques during the game, as close to the moment when you will need the skills you have visually mastered. For example, during a match the tennis player can instantaneously do a mental rehearsal prior to each serve.

The more familiar you become with the mental rehearsal technique, the more ways you will find to use it in your game. Be innovative and experimental to discover what works best for you.

DIRECTING THE MOVIES OF   Phase Three
MENTAL IMAGERY

Time: Three 20- to 30-minute sessions

Benefits: You will be learning complete instructions for creating mental imagery to guide your movements for peak performance.

The instructions that follow build on the relaxation and mental rehearsal skills you have mastered thus far. In this exercise you will learn to create mental imagery for complete actions in your sport. These images will act as mental models directing neuromuscular signals throughout your entire body.

Preparation

You must be proficient in the relaxation technique (Lesson 3) and in the two phases of mental rehearsal that precede this one.

Instructions

Step One: Choose the Cast

To make a complete "movie" for mental rehearsal, you will need a "hero" or "heroine"—that is, an athlete more proficient than you are, a person whose actions and form can serve as a model for further developing *your* actions and form.

Not everyone chooses professional or world-class athletes as his or her model. The *overall* performance of the person you choose need not be better than yours if they offer some skill that you wish to learn or perfect. For example, you may play tennis with a person who is about your equal in scoring but whose backhand is far superior to yours.

You will focus your attention on very specific actions. You might, for example, watch this person's body positions, the attitudes assumed, movements, the manifestation of speed, power, endurance, and so on.

Step Two: Prepare the Camera

The same principles that apply in the first two phases of mental rehearsal also apply here. You must be deeply relaxed, and you must be mentally receptive to what you are seeing, hearing, and feeling.

Step Three: Choose the Location

Where will you shoot your movie? What is your star's best camera angle? Where does the star excel? These are the practical issues that you will need to address. If the star of your movie frequently works out with you, the location will be no problem. The gym, track, pool, or court where you are ordinarily together will be your location. If your model is a famous sports figure, the problem is more difficult. Films will help, and being a spectator at games or tournaments will also help, allowing you to study actual movements in detail.

A word about "camera angle": your interest in other athletes may involve a single movement, as we have already discussed. For example, you may want to focus on footwork in a specific movement, how a golfer holds her club, how a tennis player raises his shoulder to serve, or you may even try to discern what the person does to maintain concentration during a game. Make certain you know exactly what you want from your hero or heroine. Refer to your goal charts (Lesson 2) if you need guidance in defining the needs.

Step Four: Make the Movie

Once you have established your location, your star is in place, and you have decided on which movement you are going to focus, the rest will come naturally.

In a relaxed state, focus your attention on your model. As you learned to do in Phases One and Two, pay particular attention to the sensory details associated with your star's actions. You may need to watch the same movements many times, focusing on the movement of an arm, leg, or even the total body, until you have a very clear, in-focus picture in your mind.

Each time you "shoot," close your eyes and see how much of the movie you can see in your mind's eye. (If you have learned Phases One and Two of this lesson, you will be able to do this after two or three shootings.)

As in Lesson 2, choose a name for the movie in order to mentally catalogue and retrieve the film whenever you need it.

Step Five: Rehearse with the Movies

The best way to use your mental movies is in practice rather than in competition. The process is exactly the same as in Phase Two—run the movie in your mind just prior to actually performing the activity. Feel the energy in your muscles, and then put yourself into the action, duplicating in real life the actions you have recorded in your mental movie.

Bill Russell said he discovered at times that his movies were incomplete, that he had missed some small detail the first time around. Should you discover that you cannot re-create the mental scenes in real life because of a missing detail or because you find that you don't know exactly what to do with a particular part of your body, go back on location and shoot new film, giving extra attention to those areas of the body about which you want to acquire more information.

At times during mental rehearsal you may grow restless and feel a need to move around. This occurs because the visualization process is sending impulses to the muscles, as it is supposed to do, and restlessness is thus proof that the mental rehearsal process is working. If restlessness should occur, simply get up and walk around or act out the visualization.

SUMMARY

You now have the basic mental rehearsal skills for developing high levels of performance. In this three-phase lesson you have focused most of your attention on physical factors, although thoughts and feelings associated with movements have also been discussed. In the following lesson, Athletic Poise, you will learn about arousal states—what they are, how they supply power and energy, and how you can use them to create and maintain peak performance levels.

APPLICATIONS FOR THIS LESSON
OUTSIDE SPORTS

Career/Business: In the same way that athletes mentally rehearse important competitions, you can mentally rehearse interviews, staff presentations, or new organizational procedures. The same mental rehearsal process is also invaluable for creating an internal sense of a future goal, as we described in Lesson 2 on goal-setting.

For example, in the process of developing and marketing a new product, mental rehearsal has numerous applications: a mental image of the product is essential for describing what you wish to develop to designers and engineers; a mental image of a marketing plan will aid not only in putting together a promotional package but also in directing design and packaging decisions; and a mental image of distribution and shipping procedures helps in all the above decisions as well as in pricing the product and in identifying known markets. In addition, miscellaneous mental rehearsals provide guidelines for financing the development of the product, reorganizing employees, and so forth.

In most companies top executives have clear but not necessarily highly detailed mental images of the overall activities of their companies. It is up to various department heads and supervisors to work out the finer details and daily routines. For maximum productivity, each responsible person consciously develops a clear mental image of the activities he or she will be directing, in concert with other departments within the organization.

Personal: Mental rehearsal serves you in your personal life in a variety of ways. In affirming educational goals, your mental rehearsal of how you will be living your life in the future guides your choices and actions in the same way that mentally rehearsing an athletic goal guides your choices and actions in sports. Mental rehearsals also provide frameworks for guiding you in planning vacations, improving personal relationships, and even in redecorating your work or living space.

Remember, clear mental rehearsals act as neuromuscular *templates* or *models,* precisely directing your thoughts and feelings. These mental rehearsals help you keep focused in your efforts, maximizing the chances of achieving your goals in the shortest period of time with a minimal output of energy.

ATHLETIC POISE

Maintaining Peak
Performance Feelings

If you are relaxing and subconsciously thinking about your coming race, you are going to perform at just about 100 percent efficiency.

Mark Spitz
winner of seven Olympic
gold medals

Athletic poise is the ability to recognize and maintain a particular state of psychological readiness, a mental preparedness that athletes and sports psychologists acknowledge as being a prerequisite to peak performance. Most high-level athletes in the United States say that they are able to create and maintain this state even when the pressure of competition is very high. They also report that they have learned athletic poise unconsciously or through trial and error and that they are not usually aware of doing anything special to achieve or maintain this important performance state.

The Soviets have demonstrated that this performance state can be systematically taught. Following the Soviets' philosophy, you can develop athletic poise by: becoming aware of the ideal performance state; getting in touch with your own experiences in this state; and mentally rehearsing psychological readiness as part of preparing for competition.

SECRETS OF THE POISED ATHLETE

Payton Jordan, perhaps America's most successful Olympic track-and-field coach, has called discus thrower Al Oerter one of the "most mentally poised" athletes he has ever met. Oerter had the ability to maintain, in himself, what Soviet sports psychologist V. A. Romanov has identified as "optimal psychological readiness" under the most intense pressures of competition. I understood what Jordan meant when I spoke with Oerter following his victory at the 1968 Olympic games, held in Mexico City, where he won his fourth gold medal, establishing a new world record in the discus with a throw of 212 feet, 6½ inches. At that time, Oerter was thirty-two years old, already held three gold medals, and was the first man in history to break 200 feet in Olympic discus competition.

I had been familiar with Oerter's athletic capabilities for a number of years. In 1967, we were both employed at the Grumman Aerospace Corporation and had worked out in our off-hours at a gym across the street from Grumman. Even watching Oerter work out, I was always aware of his sense of reserve and self-mastery. He knew himself well, both mentally and physically, and he had an acceptance of his own personal idiosyncrasies. He was patient about his own limitations, though he was always pushing beyond them. He had a great ability to calmly self-criticize and self-correct. Oerter seemed to recognize fully his emotions as a source of power and inspiration that contributed to his abilities, and he knew how to direct his emotions for maximum benefit.

Maintaining the ideal performance state was not—at least for Oerter—a complicated process. He described his own athletic poise as "the ability to step outside yourself" and to calmly ask how you can correct or improve your performance. He did not struggle with his own ego to do this; such a struggle can lead to "choking" or to caving in under pressure. Oerter reflected that there was clearly a state of mind that made it possible for him to perform at the highest levels of which he was capable, but he expressed this in a very casual way: "As long as I can concentrate and remain somewhat calm, I can normally do very well."

In an article published in *Sports* journal, psychologist James Loehr reported that in hundreds of interviews with peak performing athletes, it became apparent that very few were conscious of what Loehr called the "optimal performance state" and that they were only "vaguely aware of an ideal internal climate for performing." Nevertheless, he and other researchers have discovered that performance is directly affected by one's ability to create and maintain this state voluntarily.

Even after interviewing large numbers of peak performers and listening to them tell about their own techniques for creating the ideal internal climate, I am still astounded at how simple they can make it sound. Indeed, once learned it is easy. As my training partner Marilyn King once told me: "When I reach a troubled place or feel stuck, I immediately reflect on my past athletic experiences and what worked for me then." What could be simpler than that? Digging deeper, we see that the process so simply described is actually very complex.

The opinion of most researchers is that top-level athletes generally control this optimal performance state subconsciously and automatically. Loehr has said that "the *gifted* athletes seem to be able to perfect these techniques quickly on their own, while most [other] athletes need specific training techniques to accelerate their acquisition of these skills."

Loehr compiled information from a large cross section of peak performers in a variety of sports, using both oral and written interviews, and he determined the following:

1. An ideal internal psychological climate exists for every athlete.
2. When an athlete feels right, performance is right.
3. The level of performance is a direct reflection of the way one feels inside.
4. Performing toward the upper range of one's potential is a natural consequence of the right kind of internal feeling occurring at the right time.

5. The elements of the ideal performance state are fundamentally the same for all athletes and all sports.

6. The ideal performance state is most accurately described in terms of specific states of feeling experienced by individual performers.

7. Competitive toughness is essentially the ability to create and sustain the ideal performance state regardless of the circumstances of play.

The next question we must ask is, What are the feelings associated with this ideal performance state? Are they identifiable, and if so, what can an athlete do to learn to control that state? Loehr's research corroborates my own, confirming that "the ideal internal climate for performing is characterized by high-level energy intensity accompanied by a profound sense of inner calmness." The high energy and the inner calmness, rather than being two simple components, are together actually a complex of mental and physical conditions that I call *peak performance feelings.*

PEAK PERFORMANCE FEELINGS

By examining hundreds of interviews, statements and biographies of elite athletes, I was able to identify eight mental and physical conditions that athletes describe as being characteristic of the feelings they have at those moments when they are doing something extraordinarily well. These characteristics have been discussed throughout the book, but in the following paragraphs they are summarized and presented all together. The athletes have feelings of being:

1. *Mentally relaxed.* Of all the feeling states examined, a sense of inner calm is by far the most frequently mentioned. Along with this inner calm, athletes often report feeling a sense of time being slowed down and having a high degree of concentration. By contrast, a loss of con-

centration, a sense of everything happening too fast, and a sense of things being out of control are associated with mental tension.

2. *Physically relaxed.* Feeling that the muscles are loose, with movements fluid, precise, and sure, is closely linked with peak performance.

3. *Confident and optimistic, with a generally positive outlook.* A feeling of self-confidence, a positive attitude, or an inner sense of optimism about being able to perform well is reported as a key factor that determines whether the athlete can transform a potentially threatening athletic challenge into a success while maintaining poise.

4. *Focused on the present.* Athletes report having a sense of mind-body integration or of harmony between mental and physical functions, and of not having any thoughts or feelings about the past or future. (Learning to be "in the present" is one of the key disciplines taught in the martial arts.) When completely focused on the present, logical and analytical processes are suspended, and as this occurs the athlete has the sense that all actions are occurring automatically and effortlessly.

5. *Highly energized.* Words such as *joy, ecstasy, intensity,* and *power* are frequently used to describe this highly energized state. Although fear, anxiety, and even rage have been traditionally associated with high performance levels, these feelings were rarely mentioned as contributing in any way to this high energy state.

6. *Extraordinary awareness.* Athletes almost universally describe a state of mind in which they are acutely aware of their bodies and of the athletes around them and have an uncanny ability to anticipate correctly other athletes' moves and respond effectively to them. This awareness is closely related to the state of being focused on the present (see 4, above).

7. *In Control.* Although athletes report a feeling of being in control, the control described is largely subconscious. There

appears to be no deliberate effort at the moment of peak performance to *exert* control over the situations around them or over other people, but there is a definite sense of being able to make all the right moves, with the results being exactly what they intended.

8. *In the "cocoon."* The word *cocoon* has been used for many years to describe the sense of being insulated from the anxiety or fear ordinarily associated with particularly challenging athletic situations, which would normally arouse fight-or-flight responses. Being in this cocoon, the athlete was able to avoid the loss of concentration, the accelerated, tight-muscled, out-of-control feelings commonly associated with the fight-or-flight response.

A number of words and phrases are used to describe the overall experience when mental and physical elements have come together to produce a peak performance: being "hot" or "in the groove" or finding the "sweet spot," and so on. Sportswriter John Jerome described some of the benefits enjoyed at such moments: "When an athlete is hitting the internal sweet spots—when the timing is right and the motion is smooth— the skills levels are higher, the athletic motions quicker, more forceful, more accurate. . . . The athlete is performing "within" himself or herself, under control, within the limits to motion beyond which human tissue is overstressed. And there is one more advantage to this smooth-running vision of athletics: endurance."

In summarizing the research of a number of other psychologists, Loehr has said: "Feelings and emotions create energy and force.* Feelings and emotions trigger psychological arousal, and the right combination of feelings produces the

---

*In his research of mental imagery at SyberVision, Inc., Steve DeVore has begun exploring the powers of "electromagnetic waveforms" produced by thoughts and visualizations. In 1982, he reported at a seminar at Stanford University that "electromagnetic waveforms" may attract us to opportunities for success. Although research to date is inconclusive, DeVore has raised some thought-provoking questions about the nature of our mental processes.

kind of physiological arousal that contributes to the high-level performance."

In contrast to performing while in this peak performance state, Loehr said, "attempting to perform well in the presence of the wrong emotional climate is in many ways analogous to planting a seed in frozen soil. The potential of the seed cannot manifest itself until the conditions of temperature, moisture, and so on, are optimal."

It is essential to understand the relationships between feelings, energy, and the ability to concentrate on the present with the ability to perform. In Figure 5–1, The Peak Performance Compass, you will find a graphic presentation of these relationships.

In the peak performance segment (at the top of the figure), you will find those components that will direct you toward peak performance in whatever you do. Feelings in this section are positive—that is, the athlete enters the event with a high expectation of success. Feelings are directed toward performing well rather than on showing up another player, proving a point, or in some way expressing anger or hostility. At the same time, attention is focused on the present performance rather than on events in the past or future. Finally, the athlete has the feeling of possessing great energy and of having the ability to channel that energy into the performance.

In both the average performance areas to the left and right of the peak performance section you will find a shifting focus of attention. Instead of focusing directly on performance in the present, the athlete is focusing either sporadically or constantly on something in the past (such as a past error or failure), or on something in the future (such as the fear of being unable to meet the next challenge). The attentional focus may also be diminished by anger toward another player, causing an investment of more attention on settling a personal score rather than on the performance itself.

In the average performance segment on the left, you will note a medium-to-varying energy level. Energy reserves are diminished, possibly as a result of slight depression, distraction,

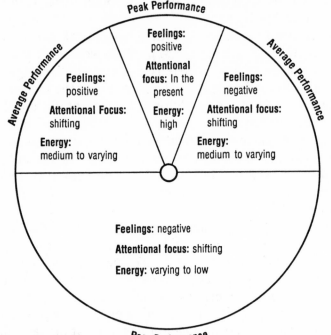

Figure 5–1 The Peak Performance Compass. Each of us has within us a sense of how it feels to be in the state of psychological readiness that leads to peak performance. For elite athletes, this sense is highly developed and acts as a compass, or homing device that tells them not only when they are on course, but also when they are off course and what needs to be corrected. This figure, as well as the text explanation, will help you develop this homing device in yourself.

or fatigue. Trouble arises not when the energy level is somewhat reduced but when the athlete cannot *depend* on it—that is, when it is medium to high at one moment, low the next, and high or medium at the beginning of a play, only to drop halfway through. The most significant difference between the two average performance segments is in the feelings which are positive on the left and negative on the right.

In neither Loehr's research nor in mine is there evidence of a peak performance when negative emotions are present, *regardless of the attentional focus or energy levels*. Note, however, that short bursts of high energy and optimal performance are occasionally reported by players in team sports, where anger provoked by another player may briefly stimulate an athlete. But as both Rushall and Kauss have found, this burst of energy is a result of the adrenaline rush associated with the fight-or-flight response, and it is highly unpredictable and frequently followed by a sense of confusion or even fatigue.

In the poor performance segment, at the bottom of the compass, we find a combination of the worst components: negative feelings (such as anger, fear, vengefulness, and so on), low energy (associated here with feelings of defeat, laziness, tiredness, depression, or a sense of being burned out), and the inability to focus attention. The shifting of attention is accompanied by an illusion of accelerated time, and, though the athlete may continue to go through the motions, there may be a distinct decrease in volition.

THREE STEPS TO ATHLETIC POISE

To achieve athletic poise, you must evaluate your state of psychological readiness and self-correct when that state is not optimal. You accomplish this through a three-step process:

Step One. Begin by knowing the characteristics of psychological readiness, the eight peak performance feelings and the components illustrated in The Peak Performance Compass (Figure 5–1), and by being able to recognize them in yourself (Figure 5–2, Neurophysiological Cues).

Step Two. Having evaluated yourself using the Peak Performance Feelings Rating Sheet (Figure 5–3), you will know which skills you need to develop further in order to achieve the optimal readiness state. This will be implemented by the Skills Reference Table (Figure 5–4), which follows the Peak Performance Scale instructions.

Step Three. As the first steps of athletic poise are learned, you will find yourself going through the entire process automatically—so automatically that you may be unaware of doing anything special. In order to encourage this automatic process, the peak performer learns to mentally rehearse the state of psychological readiness in the same way that performance on a physical level is rehearsed. This ability is developed in Phase Two of this lesson, called Creating an Expectation of Success.

THE PEAK PERFORMANCE SCALE   Phase One

Time: One 20-to-30-minute session
Benefits: You will learn to evaluate your peak performance state in terms of the eight peak performance feelings.

In this exercise you will rate your own past performance in accordance with the eight peak performance feelings discussed earlier in this lesson. This information will allow you to judge your mental state prior to performance so that you can consciously change that state before actually launching into the action. First, you must use the accompanying rating scale, labeled from 0 to 10. Below-average performance on this scale is in the 0-to-3 range, while average performance is in the 4-to-7 range. Peak performance occurs only in the 8-to-10 range.

Through completing a large number of ratings, you will learn that peak performance occurs only when all eight of the peak performance feeling categories fall in the 8-to-10 range. For example, the rating sheet reflecting one of the best performances of a power lifter with whom I worked looked like this:

Peak Performance Feelings	Rating
1. *Mentally relaxed*	9
2. *Physically relaxed*	10
3. *Confident/Optimistic*	10
4. *Focused on the present*	9
5. *Highly energized*	10

6. *Extraordinary awareness*   8
7. *In control*   10
8. *In the cocoon*   8

An interesting contrast to this was a rating sheet from a runner who classified herself as primarily recreational. Rating herself following a five-mile run during which she "felt like a peak performer," she submitted the following:

Peak Performance Feelings	Rating
1. *Mentally relaxed*	9
2. *Physically relaxed*	10
3. *Confident/Optimistic*	6
4. *Focused on the present*	10
5. *Highly energized*	7
6. *Extraordinary awareness*	7
7. *In control*	6
8. *In the cocoon*	9

Even though the recreational athlete did not turn in a performance that broke any records, she felt extremely good about herself and rated the run as a "peak experience" in her life.

The ratings provide an indication of where improvement is needed in order for you to become a peak performer. For example, if the recreational runner profiled wished to begin competing, she would see from her rating chart that additional time and energy must be devoted to practice for each of those categories in which she rated herself at less than 8 (Confident/Optimistic, Highly energized, Extraordinary awareness, and In control). The skills for developing these mental states have been described in earlier lessons. At the end of this exercise, you will find The Skills Reference Table, which directs you to the specific sections of the book for the skills you need.

By what criteria will you be rating yourself? The ratings are most valuable when you allow yourself to be subjective. Your purpose in this exercise is not to create a universal rating system to demonstrate how you compare with other athletes, but rather to develop your own skills of being able to step outside yourself and recognize where you need to improve.

To help yourself recognize the subjective experiences associated with each of the eight peak performance feelings categories, study Neurophysiological Cues, Figure 5–2. In each of the categories you will find cues for focusing your attention on mental and/or emotional experiences characteristic of that category. You will find when you actually begin rating yourself that you have a natural inclination for establishing numerical criteria as well as for sensing intuitively how either end of the scale might feel. And even though you may have never experienced the highest end of the scale, you will have a surprisingly *clear* sense of what it might be like to experience it!

Preparation

Make at least three copies of Figure 5–3, the Peak Performance Feelings Rating Sheet. Work on this during a time when you will not be disturbed for twenty to thirty minutes. Allow yourself to be in a relaxed state as you work.

Instructions

Step One: Rate Your Most Recent Performance

Begin by rating yourself on your most recent performance. To do this, relive the experience, recalling as vividly as you can the moments just prior to, during, and immediately following the event. Recall what kind of a day it was, whether you felt warm or cold, and so on. Focus on your senses: what you saw, what you heard, what you touched, what you smelled, and so on. Who was with you at the time?

Using Figure 5–3 to guide you, focus your attention on each of the eight categories. *Take your time.* Imagine yourself reliving the event as you are rating it. Allow yourself to feel once again the sensations associated with each of the eight

Figure 5–2 NEUROPHYSIOLOGICAL CUES OF PEAK PERFORMANCE FEELINGS

Category	Cues
1. Mentally Relaxed	Inner calm; time slowed; able to focus clearly on details in the present.
2. Physically Relaxed	Muscles loose throughout body; feelings of warmth; movements fluid; body seems to respond directly and precisely to volition.
3. Confident/Optimistic	High expectation of success; recognition of challenge and excitement in response to the idea of accepting that challenge; feelings of strength and control.
4. Focused on the Present	Sense of harmony—that is, of body and mind working together as a unit; no thoughts of past or future; a sense of body performing automatically, without conscious or deliberate mental effort.
5. Highly Energized	Associated with feelings of joy, ecstasy, intensity, and of feeling "charged" or "hot."
6. Extraordinary Awareness	An acutely sharp sense of one's whole body and its movements (perceived as physical sensations rather than as thoughts or ideas); acute awareness of other players' movements, size, physical presence, and of how these players think and feel (mental impressions rather than analysis); ability to know what other players are going to do even before they do it; a sensation of being completely in harmony with one's environment.
7. In Control	Body seems to be automatically doing exactly what you want it to do; mind seems to respond to the environment and to process all information from it in the most effficient and appropriate ways possible; no sense of exerting or imposing control, though everything is happening as you wish it to.
8. In the Cocoon	Feelings of being in an envelope, with complete access to all one's powers and skills; feelings of detachment from external environment, even though acutely aware of everything associated with your performance; not reacting to events that detract from the performance; a feeling of euphoric awareness and of containment of one's skills and power; a feeling of invulnerability.

Figure 5-3   PEAK PERFORMANCE FEELINGS RATING SHEET

Category	0	1	2	3	4	5	6	7	8	9	10
1. Mentally Relaxed											
2. Physically Relaxed											
3. Confident/Optimistic											
4. Focused on the Present											
5. Highly Energized											
6. Extraordinary Awareness											
7. In Control											
8. In the Cocoon											

categories, each of the eight peak performance feelings. For example, when you focus on mental relaxation, do you feel an inner calm? A sense of time being slowed? An ability to calmly focus on details?

In a moment you will have a clear impression of the mental relaxation you experienced for this event. As you hold that impression in your mind, say to yourself, "Give me a number to rate this category." Write down, on the rating sheet, the first number that comes to your mind regarding your performance.

Do not worry about analyzing why you are rating yourself. Simply write whatever number comes to mind as you relive the experience. Rate each of the eight categories.

Step Two: Rate Your Worst Performance

To rate your worst performance, follow the same instructions as for step one. When doing so, keep in mind that most athletes, not wishing to dwell on what they consider to be past failures, have a tendency to skip lightly over this part of the exercise, automatically giving themselves low ratings in all categories without attempting to relive what they were experiencing. However, the ultimate goal in doing this exercise is not to produce rating charts but to put you in touch with your own feelings, so that you will really know the difference between *best* and *worst* in judging psychological readiness and in making any necessary adjustments before or during an actual performance.

Step Three: Rate Your Best Performance
Following the same instructions as in steps one and two, rate
yourself on your best performance.

Step Four: Use the Skills Reference Table
Having completed three rating sheets, look for the areas in
which you most consistently rate below the 8-to-10 range. For
example, you may discover that you consistently rate low in
being in control and having confidence. Turn to Figure 5–4,
the Skills Reference Table, and seek those areas in which you
need work. The lesson/phase number column then supplies you
with numbers referring to the exercises (lesson number first;
exercise number next) in the book that will help you to develop
the skills you need for improving your performance. The comments in the third column of the table provide capsule explanations of how the skills you need will contribute to your
increased performance capabilities.

Discussion
As you go over the Skills Reference Table, you may notice
what appear to be overlappings and/or duplications in the les-
son/phase number column as well as in the comments column.
For example, the exercises for developing mental relaxation
are duplicates of the exercises for developing physical relaxation. You will recall from Lesson 3 that mind and body are so
tightly interwoven that an idea will be reflected in muscular
responses, and relaxation of muscle fibers will be reflected in
a relaxed mental/emotional state. After working with athletes
on mental training for a number of years, I have become aware
of the arbitrary nature of separating one skill from another—
yet it is this separation that finally makes the teaching of these
skills possible.

After you have developed skills in all the areas presented
in this book, you will begin to appreciate how they all come
together in an orchestrated manner, in part because of their
overlapping nature. You will experience how your development
of voluntary relaxation, for example, enhances positive feel-

Figure 5–4 SKILLS REFERENCE TABLE

Peak Performance Feelings	Lesson/Phase Number	Comments
1) Mentally Relaxed	3:1/3:3	This component is dependent both on your ability to recognize tension and on your ability to voluntarily create and maintain a relaxed state.
2) Physically Relaxed	3:1/3:2/3:3	Same as above, since neurophysiologists tell us that mental and physical relaxation are the same. In addition, breathing exercises can quickly relieve tension prior to or during an athletic performance without reducing the positive excitement that increases performance ability.
3) Confident/Optimistic	1:1/1:2/1:3/5:2	These positive emotions depend on clearly knowing you are engaged in an activity in which you experience high volitional impact. It will also be affected by your physical conditioning and by your ability to maintain overall athletic poise.
4) Focused on the Present	1:3/3:1/3:2/3:3/4:3	Autogenic training, combined with mental rehearsal, brings the mind in harmony with the physical activity at the time of execution; mental rehearsal leaves little room for distraction by thoughts, activities outside the performance focus, and so on. Maintaining focus and concentration is also dependent on your being engaged in what for you are high-volitional-impact activities and on your working toward goals with high expectation of success.
5) Highly Energized	1:2/1:3/3:3/5:2	Sleep and nutrition are essential for high energy in athletics, of course, but beyond that, in mental training, we discover that having positive emotions and being focused on the present are also associated with high energy. All the lessons through which these (positive emotions and focus) are achieved are, thus, essential.

Figure 5-4 SKILLS *(continued)*

Peak Performance Feelings	Lesson/Phase Number	Comments
6) Extraordinary Awareness	1:3/3:3/4:3	The combination of being engaged in an activity that has high volitional impact for you, being relaxed and open to that experience, and establishing harmony between your mental image of the activity and the activity itself creates a sense of acute awareness of every detail of the physical performance.
7) In Control	1:3/3:3/4:3	As in extraordinary awareness, control comes about through a combination of being engaged in activities that have high volitional impact, being relaxed and open to the experience, and having mentally rehearsed the activity so that mind and body seem to respond directly to your wishes. In addition, prolonged practice through physical conditioning increases the *sense* of control as well as the physical fact of control.
8) In the Cocoon	1:3/3:3/4:3/5:2	The cocoon, as described by many athletes, constitutes an extremely high level of concentration, achieved by focusing all of their attention, energy, and expectation of success on an activity that deeply interests them.

ings, smooth and precise muscular movements, and extraordinary awareness. Just as with the training of a very inspired team, the development of each individual part contributes to the whole in ways that are frequently impossible to trace, the total benefits rippling through every area, increasing power and enhancing overall performance.

CREATING AN EXPECTATION OF SUCCESS   Phase Two

Time: One 20-minute session (the number of sessions will vary according to the individual)

Benefits: Feelings of success activate previously developed mental skills of the peak performer. The ability to activate these feelings under pressure constitutes athletic poise. Although it is related to Lesson 1, in which you identified volitional patterns in your life, this new exercise helps you focus specifically on the feelings of success.

As you develop peak performance skills you will find that the more adept you become in each skill, the more they seem to come together not as separate skills to be applied one at a time, but as a larger attitude—*poise*—that you assume the moment you engage in an athletic activity.

Peak performers distinguish themselves from those who merely do well by having a particularly strong expectation of success that represents the coming together of both the mental and physical skills in the elite athlete. Moreover, these athletes are able to draw on the emotional contents of previous experiences of success, and this reliving of the emotional content activates previously developed mental skills (such as relaxation, mental rehearsal, and others described in this book). A graphic example of this process was presented to me during a discussion I had with Al Oerter shortly after he won his fourth Olympic gold medal.

Going into the 1968 Olympics, Oerter was not the favorite.

The favorite that year was his teammate Jay Sylvester, who then held the world record in the discus.

Oerter, by his own admission, was not doing well in the finals. He was having difficulty focusing on the present, his control was off, and his confidence was low. At that moment, he says, he re-created in his mind the emotions he had felt during and immediately following his past victories. His recall of these feelings was vivid. He concentrated on his experiences of success, taking time to recapture the emotions he had felt and reexperience them in their original intensity and depth. Slowly, he felt the high energy and excitement of success swelling within him. Within moments he had regained his poise completely, and the throw he then made won him the gold.

Some people deny that they have past experiences of success upon which to draw. But after working with literally thousands of people, I assure you that *everyone* has a success upon which to build. This experiece may or may not be athletic; the exact content is not as important as the quality of the experience that comes with knowing that you have done something extremely well.

To create an expectation of success, you must dip into your memory and re-create vivid mental images of your past moments of success. It may be difficult the first time you do this to restore the feelings of success to their original vividness and power, but with each practice session it will become easier for you to jog your memory and to vividly relive the experience. In Lesson 1, you explored moments from your past when you experienced success. There you were being asked to explore the kinds of experiences that have high volitional impact for you. In *this* exercise, however, you are to focus specifically on feelings of success. (It may be helpful for you to review the clusters you assembled in Lesson 1.)

Note that the expectation of success is not created in a single session but rather through a series of sessions. Over time—varying from one or two sessions for those who are already in touch with their feelings of success to a dozen or more sessions for those who are in the habit of dwelling on past failures rather than successes—the creation of an expectation of success becomes nearly automatic, requiring little more than the word *success* to set a vivid memory in motion.

What do you do if you have just begun a sport and have no successes in that sport upon which to build? I cannot emphasize this point strongly enough: again, it is *not the specific event* that matters but the *quality of the experience* of success that you will be seeking.

Now begin to create your expectation of success.

Preparation
Work during a time when you will not be disturbed for at least twenty minutes. Put yourself in a deeply relaxed state, using the skills you learned in Lesson 3.

Instructions
Let yourself go back to a time when you did something extraordinarily well. This may be something from your recent past or from your childhood. It may be the memory of an athletic event or of something you accomplished in your work, at home, in recreation, in school.

Put yourself completely into the memory. How did you feel? Were you excited? Feel that excitement once again, just as though you were experiencing it for the first time.

Did you feel happy about sharing your success with others around you? If so, recall any laudatory remarks about your accomplishment.

Were you aware of any sounds around you? What did you see that you particularly associate with this moment of success?

How did your body feel? Go over your body, from head to foot, recalling everything you felt.

What, if anything, did you taste or smell?

Focus directly on your emotions. Without giving a name to these feelings, let yourself experience them again.

Take a deep breath. Hold it for five seconds, then exhale slowly and evenly. This simple technique helps you to relax and focus. As you exhale, relive your memory of success, allowing yourself to intensify any emotions associated with this moment.

Take another deep breath. Hold it for five seconds. Exhale. Again, let yourself feel the emotions of the successful moment.

To further intensify your memories of this success, refocus on each of your senses and explore the details you perceive. Make a note of as many details of sight, sound, and smell as you can. Take your time. Explore what you see, feel, taste, touch. Let yourself fully enjoy all these sensory proofs of this moment of success.

After you have vividly recalled your moment of success, notice how you feel both mentally and physically. Are you relaxed? Are you able to easily focus on the present? Are you more aware than usual of things going on around you? Check the Peak Performance Compass (Figure 5–1) to see how focused on the peak performance segment you are at this moment.

Discussion

Make it a practice to turn your attention to those feelings you have discovered in past moments of success at least twice a day. The purpose is to develop a habit of thinking in terms of success. Most of us, as Abraham Maslow has pointed out, are far more habituated to looking for our errors than to giving ourselves credit for our accomplishments. Although our objective in dwelling on failure may be to identify our errors so we can self-correct and ultimately improve performance, the end result is to separate ourselves from those experiences that allow us to identify success. We forget how it feels to be successful.

Having been fully in touch with feelings of success and having developed the habit of recalling these feelings frequently, recognize that with the ability to do these things you can mentally rehearse to create these feelings prior to or during any performance, just as you mentally rehearse movements or plays (Lesson 4). *Expect* success. Relive it within you, and you will discover the power of peak performance magic occurring in the real world what a short time before had been only imaginary.

SUMMARY

You have learned the secrets of athletic poise, of being able to evaluate your feelings prior to and during a performance, and of self-correcting in order to put yourself into a winning frame of mind. The skills you have developed through the two exercises in this lesson will allow you to fine-tune your awareness of all the peak performance skills presented in this book and to apply them directly and instantly as integral parts of your athletic performance. In the exercise on creating an expectation of success, you learned a process for bringing all the skills of the peak performer into a single image or experience. The ability to create or mentally rehearse this expectation of success is your way of orchestrating the numerous skills you have mastered on a more individualized basis.

APPLICATIONS FOR THIS LESSON OUTSIDE SPORTS

Career/Business: In the highly competitive environment of business, most peak performers report that one's greatest asset is frequently the ability to maintain a state of "psychological readiness" identical to the one described in this lesson for athletes. Your recognition of this state of readiness can make the difference between peak performance and merely doing well in important presentations to staff members, in contract negotiations, and in instituting change where your efforts are being met with resistance. To make full use of the skills described in this lesson, use the image of the athlete confronted by a challenging competition as your metaphor for the challenge you face in your career or business. Look upon yourself as the highly accomplished athlete in your own brand of the Olympics and maintain your poise, applying the same methods you've learned in this lesson.

    Personal: Whenever you feel that you are or recognize that soon you will be in a situation that is to be unusually demanding, go back to the metaphor in which you picture yourself as the champion athlete confronting a challenging task. Take the time to get and hold that image steadily in your mind, and feel it in your body. Then you can maintain your *personal poise* at a much higher level as you make choices and commit yourself to actions that will result in your meeting the challenge and achieving your desired goal.

Lesson 6

LETTING GO

Turning Over the Controls to Your
Internal Peak Performer

There is generally not any conscious thought; it's all instinct, and practice takes over.

—Cindy Nelson
member of the
U.S. ski team

In the final moments before a game, successful athletes self-induce (consciously or unconsciously) a mental state akin to amnesia, wherein they lose all conscious thought of what has been learned about how to use the mind and body. Some athletes have described this as "playing in a trance" or "going on automatic pilot" or "letting go." I prefer the last term, since it is the most accurate of these three phrases. This lesson, Letting Go, is the culmination of the Peak Performance Training Program, bringing together in a new form all the skills you have developed thus far.

DREAMS OF SUCCESS

Again and again, elite athletes state that peak performance is not a *common* act of will. In his study of the peak experience, Abraham Maslow explained that "the will does not interfere. It is held in abeyance. It receives and doesn't demand. We cannot command the peak experience. It happens *to* us."

179

Although we may not be able to command peak performance, as Maslow tells us, it can be *orchestrated* in sports. The difference is found in the manner in which athletes actualize themselves.

Rather than finding that elite athletes succeed because they exert conscious control of body and mind, we discover that it is just the opposite. Though they may exert control in the form of self-discipline and a search for knowledge during the training phase, during the actual performance stage there is a sense of abandonment. One of the more notable statements, in my opinion, was made by Catfish Hunter after he pitched a perfect game against the Minnesota Twins in 1968. Hunter told reporters, "It was like a dream. I was going on like I was in a daze. I never thought about it the whole time."

In the Soviet literature, much is made of the preparation stage, prior to athletic performance, but very little attention has been given to the letting-go stage. It is in this area, more than in other parts of mental training, that the Americans have taken the lead, though the issue of letting go has been oversimplified by some of our own sports psychologists.

Letting go is ineffective unless it is preceded by both physical conditioning and mental training. There is no substitute for the hard work and self-discipline that go into athletic training, but without the ability to let go, the discipline invested can actually be counterproductive.

In Timothy Gallwey's *Inner Game of Tennis,* an interesting work on letting go in sports, the author quoted the Zen master D. T. Suzuki, who said, "Great works are done when [one] is not calculating and thinking." Elaborating on this, Gallwey wrote:

> When a tennis player is "on his game," he's not thinking about how, when, or even where to hit the ball. He's not *trying* to hit the ball, and after the shot he doesn't think about how badly or how well he made contact. The ball seems to be hit through an automatic process that doesn't require thought. There may be an awareness of the sight, sound, and feel of the ball, and even of the tactical situation, but the player just seems to *know* without thinking what to do.

For Gallwey, this state of detachment is largely a matter of "letting go of judgment" about the game. This does not mean ignoring one's errors but instead "seeing events as they are and not adding anything to them." Hanging judgment labels on your own performance ("I really flubbed that one"; "I have a weak backhand"), claims Gallwey, "leads to emotional reactions and then to tightness, trying too hard, self-condemnation, etc."

Basketball coach Stan Kellner observed, similarly, that "once competition begins the athlete's automatic mind takes over. There is little conscious thinking." I am reminded here of former football great O. J. Simpson, who is quoted as having said, "Thinking . . . is what gets you caught from behind." Simpson said that, before games, "my biggest thing is to clear my mind. . . . I'm not thinking about anything, so hopefully I'm thinking about everything. Pulling in what I need to pull in. You just react instead of consciously thinking about it."

According to Kellner, "The player who thinks too much while playing inhibits himself. Play must be automatic, natural, and spontaneous." Kellner identifies four steps for achieving this performance state:

1. Relaxing the mind and body.
2. Discovering the power of mental pictures.
3. Improving the concentration by holding the mental picture of the desired end result for a few seconds.
4. Learning to "let it happen" rather than trying to "make it happen."

All four of these steps should be familiar to you, since they are the key skills of the Peak Performance Training Program. In a five-year study in Delaware Valley, the Association for the Advancement of Sports Potential found that the more effectively one could achieve a state of "relaxed attentiveness" (created through exercises corresponding with the above four points), "the more efficient would the movements become." Reporting on the association's research, Maurie D. Pressman explained the process of letting go in terms of right and left brain functions:

> The dominant side of the brain (the left side in right-handed people) is given to thinking, to language, to details, and to building up small efforts and small details into a larger picture, a larger gestalt. The nondominant side of the brain (the right side of the brain in right-handed people), on the other hand, is very much given to the perception of whole movements, whole ideas, gestalts; it is very much given to pictures rather than words, very much given to music rather than ideas. Therefore, inhibiting or suspending the functions of the left side of the brain, the dominant brain, frees the right side to take over. . . . In a state of focused consciousness, therefore, imagery is more vivid, rehearsal of programs is more effective, and the cultivation of positive attitudes is also much more assured. . . . Additionally, by diminishing the extra edge of tension . . . we essentially unbind the muscles, allowing the performance to flow more freely. We believe that insofar as we suspend the functions of the left side of the brain, we release the personality to flow into its activity, unselfconsciously and with smoother coordination.

Sports psychologists Evelyn Hall and Charles Hardy, in an address to the Fifth World Sport Psychology Congress in Ottawa, Canada (1981), further clarified this same point, agreeing with Pressman's analysis: "When participants think, analyze, and verbalize excessively during performance, they may suffer from what is commonly known as 'paralysis by analysis.'" Hall and Hardy also said, "Since the right hemisphere has a tremendous potential in recognizing and manipulating complex patterns and making split decisions in sport, its abilities should be strengthened and reinforced." Their prescription, if you will, was that the best performances could be achieved not by focusing on the past or the future (left brain dominance) but by focusing on the present moment (right brain dominance) through the disciplined application of the techniques of relaxation, mental rehearsal, and the creation of mental imagery.

In exploring the state of mind associated with letting go,

many sports psychologists (Ravizza 1977, Csikszentmihalyi 1979, Romen 1976, Loehr 1983, Hickman 1981, Suinn 1976) agree that words and phrases such as *automatic, unconscious, without thought,* and *focus on the present* characterize the state of mind experienced by athletes at moments of peak performance. Lee Pulos told me, "There seems to be a much greater and expanded range of abilities available when a person can shift from conscious to the more natural or subconscious linking of mind and body." This linking of mind and body is achieved through relaxation, mental rehearsal, mental imagery, and, finally, letting go.

HOW LETTING GO LOOKS AND FEELS

How does letting go look and feel? What is it like to experience it? These are key questions I am asked by athletes, coaches, and others attending my workshops. Here is a composite description compiled from hundreds of statements by peak performers who have themselves experienced this state of mind hundreds of times:

> All at once it seems as though everything is working for me. There is no sense of *needing to do* anything. My actions unfold as they do in pleasant dreams, though my body may be putting out great efforts. I have no thoughts about what I should do or how I should do it. Everything is happening automatically, as though I have tuned myself in on a radio beam that directs my nervous system so that it works in synchronization with everything in and around me. I feel insulated from all distractions. Time disappears, and even though I know the speed of actions taking place around me, I feel I have all the time I need to respond accurately and well. I am so completely involved in the action that there is not even a question of confidence or the lack of it. There are no issues such as worries about failure or feelings of fatigue. Even such feelings as momentary fear appear to serve me, changing automatically into positive forces. Success is not an issue, though at the same time it seems natural and easy to achieve. I feel strangely detached from what I am doing

even while I am completely in touch with everything, at one with my actions. The whole issue around mind and body separation seems to dissolve, really, as I feel as though both are responding perfectly to my own wishes and inner promptings. I am acutely aware of colors, sounds, the presence of people around me, the feeling of being a source of power and energy in this moment in time. It is a trancelike state, but I feel totally in touch with everything around me, with everything within me, as though the usual barriers between me and the outside world have been pulled away, and I am completely *at one* with myself and the physical world with which I am interacting. It is a wonderful feeling, crisp, full of joy, more *real* than the everyday world, going very deep, an experience that rewards me many times over for all the effort I have put into my sport.

There is a misperception about the meaning of letting go that has filtered down to the public through the media; somehow, letting go has become equated with being "laid back" or with letting "whatever happens happen," or with other phrases meaning the relinquishing of all responsibility to fate.

In actual practice, nothing could be further from the truth. Peak performing athletes fully recognize their own investment and responsibility both to that investment and to their teammates, if they happen to be engaged in a group effort. A more accurate view of letting go is that after training mind and body, the athlete learns to trust the complex subconscious mechanisms that ultimately determine peak performance, and out of that trust he or she is able to relinquish the conscious or willful controls that inhibit these subtler processes.

HOW TO LET GO

How do we let go? Most peak performers are not fully aware of doing anything special to induce the state of mind that allows them to let go. Cindy Nelson, member of the U.S. ski team, stated in the March 1983 issue of *Women's Sports* that "there is generally not any *conscious* thought, it's all instinct, and practice takes over." But this, of course, does not tell us *how—*

how one stops thinking of what should be done. Sports literature provides some hints of what athletes do to achieve this important state of mind. Golf professional Jane Blalock said, "I go into the locker room and find a corner by myself and just sit there. I try to achieve a peaceful state of nothingness that will carry over onto the golf course. If I get that feeling of quiet and obliviousness within myself, I feel I can't lose."

The state that Blalock described appears to coincide with what we know of meditative practices in the martial arts, which, as you will recall from earlier in this book, is a root source for the Soviet athletic researchers. In the martial arts, the disciplines of Zen teach the athlete to de-emphasize the intellect and to develop the intuition to a high degree. The ultimate aim is to free the athlete from anger, illusion, and false passion. We know that meditation, as used by martial-arts practitioners, is not at all foreign to Western athletes, with sports notables such as Bill Walton and Joe Namath and even entire teams, such as the Philadelphia Phillies and the Detroit Tigers, having included this practice in their training sessions.

In meditation, stilling the mind is the central task. And in preparing oneself to let go in sports, the same stillness is required. Timothy Gallwey wrote: "The greatest efforts in sports . . . come when the mind is as still as a glass lake." For Gallwey, one of the most important skills for achieving this stillness was to focus fully on the present.

Negative thoughts are the worst impediment to focusing on the present. Negative thoughts are any thoughts that stimulate negative memories of the past or that provoke negative concerns about the future. The principal reasons for "tight performance," the opposite of letting go, fall into four categories:

1. The athlete tries too hard, performing under the impression that the harder one struggles, the better the outcome.
2. The athlete worries about past mistakes, and the fear of repeating such mistakes inhibits performance. Muscles tighten up and actions become tentative and unsure.

3. The athlete becomes overly concerned about the outcome of a game or a play, causing his or her movements to be cautious, anxious, and mechanical.

4. The athlete is overly aroused and excited and forgets that the best performances are spontaneous and natural. Excessive arousal becomes a source of stress, with the athlete feeling that every action is a life-and-death struggle. When the athlete is anxious to do the right thing, conscious of every move, his or her performance is in jeopardy.

These are left brain concerns, concerns that students of the martial arts would call "false passions." In his writings on Zen Buddhism, D. T. Suzuki lumped such concerns together with the intellect, which, he said "steps in and tries to murder" the flow, or unity, between ourselves and our actions. Although intellect certainly has its usefulness in the proper sphere, letting it interfere with the flow of action in athletics can be disastrous.

Bruce Lee prescribed specific mental imagery for ridding oneself of negative thoughts: "When such a thought enters my mind, I visualize it as being written on a piece of paper. Then I visualize myself wadding the paper into a tight ball. Then I mentally light it on fire and visualize it burning to a crisp. The negative thought is destroyed, never to enter my mind again."

In a broader sense, Zen teaches the martial artist to lose the sense of self, because that *selfness* stands between the action taking place outside you and the part of you (right brain dominance) that automatically responds to that action. Suzuki tells how, in fencing, athletes must develop what he calls a "non-interfering attitude of mind," in which they can respond to the present without the interruption caused by judging the situation, fearing, or dwelling on past errors:

> The mind then reaches the highest point of alacrity, ready to direct its attention anywhere it is needed—to the left, to the right, to all the directions as required. When your attention is engaged and arrested by the striking sword of the enemy, you lose the first opportunity of making the next move by yourself. You tarry, you think, and while this deliberation goes on, your

opponent is ready to strike you down. The thing is not to give him such a chance. You must follow the movement of the sword in the hands of the enemy, leaving your mind free to make its own countermovement without your interfering deliberation.

An attitude of noninterference allows little space between the action of your opponent (or the ground coming toward you if you are a runner, or between the bow and the target if you are an archer, and so on) and the action you take in response to it. When I studied Judo, my teacher often told us that if there is room left for even the width of a hair between two actions, this is interruption. When the hands are clapped, the sound is heard without a second's delay. Although a more dramatic example than most of us will encounter in sports, the illustration of the swordsman serves Suzuki well on this point: "If you are troubled and cogitate what to do, seeing the opponent about to strike you down, you give him room, that is, a happy chance for his deadly blow." The mind that is able to develop the noninterfering attitude, we learn, "is like a boat smoothly gliding down the rapids; in Zen, and in fencing as well, a mind of no-hesitation, no-interruption, no-mediacy, is highly valued."

FOUR STEPS TO LETTING GO

In this lesson there is a single four-step exercise that brings together all the elements that have been discussed here. This exercise completes the Peak Performance Training Program, and as you will see, it is the focal point for every skill you have developed thus far. For this reason it is also the most demanding single exercise, calling upon your ability to apply directly your newly developed skills, assembling them in a condensed version of everything you have studied in this book. You will also notice that in the instructions you are asked to create mental images based on your own experiences. This individualization of the exercise is essential: if the letting-go process is to be entirely successful, it must, once learned, appear to happen almost spontaneously, and be carried forward through its own momentum. This kind of spontaneity is encouraged by building on images from *your own experience.* Take your time with each of the steps, recognizing the importance of the personalized contribution you will be bringing in the form of your own imagery.

Letting Go

Time: One 20-minute session prior to an athletic event

Benefits: You will learn to turn off the left brain, which through its logical processes impedes physical performance, and to shift cerebral activity to right brain dominance, which directs athletic performance through imagery and other intuitive processes.

This exercise consists of a four-step process: visualizing the event, quieting your mind, ridding yourself of negative thoughts, and focusing on the present.

Once these steps are learned, they flow together as one mental skill, which you will ultimately exercise automatically. After practicing the steps and applying them over a period of weeks, athletes usually report that the process comes so naturally that they are barely aware of doing anything special.

Preparation

Prerequisite to learning the letting-go process are the abilities to relax voluntarily and to create mental imagery specifically designed to affect physical performance (Lessons 3, 4, and 5).

Instructions

Step One: Visualize the Event

From an hour to as little as fifteen minutes before you are to begin an athletic event, sit down in a quiet place and create a mental image of the activity you will be performing. Since individual needs, and the requirements of competition, will vary greatly in this, you will have to experiment with the length of time prior to the game that will work best for you. For example, if you are preparing for a run of three miles over a route you know well, try sitting down for fifteen minutes prior to your run and imagining how it will feel to run it. Along with this visualization, mentally rehearse the positive feelings you wish to feel along the way. Make complete and detailed mental images. (If you plan to run over a new route, it is best to walk, or at least drive, over the course prior to your run so that you will be able to create accurate mental images that can direct your actual run.)

While creating these images, go over them repeatedly in your mind, filling in more and more details as you go. Most people will notice that thoughts, feelings, and ideas that have nothing to do with the athletic event will intrude. When this happens, immediately put the images aside by creating a new detail for the mental rehearsal. For example, let's say that as you visualize the three-mile run you are preparing to take, you begin worrying about a conflict you are having with a co-worker on your job. When that worry arises, immediately concentrate on an image directly associated with your athletic event. For example, you might use the opportunity to visualize a particular hill on the run, or you might imagine the positive feeling you wish to experience when you finish. As you do this, you literally displace negative images with positive ones, increasing your mental concentration and making the mental imagery that will guide your actions that much more complete.

Step Two: Quiet Your Mind

As you visualize your athletic activity, your mind will become increasingly focused, turning your attention toward your athletic performance and away from the events of the day. As concentration on athletic activity increases, your mind will become calm, active only where your upcoming activity is concerned. As this focus improves, marked by the disappearance of thoughts and feelings not directly associated with your sport, stop creating the mental imagery. Trust that your mind is prepared and that the images you have created are complete.

If it is at all possible, given your surroundings, close your eyes. Some athletes like to sit in the locker room with a towel over their heads at this moment. The towel signals other people that you want to be left alone, blocks visual distractions, and also establishes a ritual, which makes the exercise easier to do.

As thoughts, ideas, or feelings of any kind—athletic or nonathletic—enter your mind, let them go. Do not entertain them. For example, let's say that as you sit quietly you remember an idea for a new play that you want to try. Ordinarily, you would get excited and either go over the details in your mind for making it work or immediately look around for someone to describe it to. Even though all this may be very useful under other circumstances, your *first priority* right now is to quiet your mind. Though it will take a deliberate effort on your part, let go of the idea; add nothing to it, and don't act upon it. Understand that if it is truly a good idea it will not be lost even though not acted upon immediately.

If you are concerned with preserving an idea that comes up at this time, create an image to use again and again for such occasions. Images that I find to be effective are: wrapping the idea in an imaginary sheet of paper and placing it in an imaginary storage area in your memory bank. Or you might imagine yourself making a film of your play with a mental camera, to be automatically committed to your memory bank. Experiment with these images and create images of your own until you have some method that comes naturally and easily.

Quiet your mind by letting all thoughts, feelings, or ideas that come to your attention be either committed to memory for later reference or fade into the distance, like paper wrappers blowing across a playing field. Meditators often imagine that thoughts, feelings, and ideas are like birds flying into your field of vision, dipping their wings to fly close, then veering off and disappearing into the distance.

Through whatever images work best for you, let your thoughts and feelings go; let them fade without allowing yourself to become involved with their substance.

Step Three: Rid Yourself of Negative Thoughts
Earlier in this lesson, we spoke of four categories of negative thoughts. We spoke also of Bruce Lee's mental image for ridding himself of these negative thoughts—that is, visualizing the negative thoughts written on paper, then visualizing wadding the paper up and burning it. Learn to use this or other visualizations to rid yourself of negative feelings prior to or during any athletic performance. Another popular image, thanks to video games, is the mental picture of Pac Man gobbling up the negative thought. Choose imagery that works, that will be effortless to create, and that can be created automatically when you need it. A good source for imagery is your work or hobbies. For instance, if you often listen to music, you might imagine that negative thoughts are on a record; you can reach out and turn down the volume control until you can't hear it anymore. Similarly, a teacher might visualize erasing the negative thought from an imaginary blackboard.

Step Four: Focus on the Present
As your mind becomes more and more clear through application of the preceding processes, allow your attention to turn increasingly toward the reality of the present moment. Focus on your senses. If there is noise around you, focus on the *quality* of the sound rather than on its meaning. This takes some practice, but it will become easy in time. Focus your attention on the loudness or softness of the sound, its rhythm, its harsh or pleasing tones. Similarly, focus your attention on the visual qualities of what you see rather than on meanings; focus on colors, textures, whether the light is bright or dark, and so on. Focus on your sense of smell and taste in similar ways. Finally, focus on your sense of touch. If you use a piece of equipment such as a ball, racket, bat, or club, hold the equipment in your hand and focus on its texture, weight, and hardness. Look at the object and study its color, its curves and straight lines, the way light relfects or doesn't reflect from its surfaces. If you are a runner, stand and feel the ground under your feet. If you are a cyclist, feel the bike wherever it makes contact with your body: your hands, your feet, your buttocks.

The key to successfully focusing on the present is learning to be attentive to your senses, to the quality of *what* you are sensing rather than your interpretation of the *meaning*.

Discussion
You have now completed the four steps that prepare you to let go. If they seem complicated to you, rest assured that after you have practiced the complete process several times, all four steps will flow together as one.

As you go out on the playing field, track, court, or wherever you engage in your sport, go trustingly. Trust that you have prepared your mind and body to function at their best. Trust that you can, at this moment, control deliberate and conscious efforts and turn the direction of your movements over to your right brain; with your right brain taking a dominant role the images you have created through mental rehearsal will operate much like the sophisticated computers that guide the course of a spacecraft on a long journey into outer space. Your "computers" are operating, and you have only to get out of the way and allow your mind and body to come together as one and function at optimal levels.

SUMMARY

The more familiar you become with this letting go exercise, the more evident it becomes that it is a shorthand version of the entire Peak Performance Training Program. This single exercise, which many athletes will find themselves doing in only a few minutes before every performance, is the orchestration of the more than twenty exercises and processes you have learned throughout this book. One athlete described the letting go exercise as being like a computer chip, about the size of a small fingernail but storing information almost too complicated to describe.

Like the computer chip, the letting go exercise is also much more powerful and effective than it first appears to be. Bear in mind that if it is to become totally effective, the prerequisites described in the beginning of the exercise must be met, and the exercise itself must be practiced until it seems to unfold automatically and naturally.

APPLICATIONS FOR THIS LESSON
OUTSIDE SPORTS

Career/Business: In business, as in sports, too much thought about past mistakes and dwelling on fears of a future outcome cause a reduction in mental and physical capabilities. When under the gun in business, one's automatic response is to work harder, to get the nose to the grindstone, to put out an increased effort. However, because the pressure to increase production normally induces a high state of tension, meeting demanding deadlines too often induces just the opposite of what is needed—a nonproductive state, or a state in which productivity is at least inhibited. An extreme example of this is when exhaustion combined with tension around deadlines results in increased numbers of errors and the counterproductive backtracking necessary to correct those errors.

In business, letting go may seem contrary to everything we've been taught in our lives, but remember what we have learned about relaxation, mental rehearsal, and athletic poise—that we work at optimal levels not when we're tense and tight but when our bodies are in a relaxed state. So what does one *let go*? Under the pressure of a deadline a great deal of energy can be expended in worry and self-doubt about meeting that deadline or being able to deliver something that is required. This is roughly parallel to the athlete's worry about winning a race. The peak performer in business, as in sports, lets go of the worry, doubt, and physical tension (the fight-or-flight response), accomplishing this by conscious relaxation (Lesson 3) and by focusing on the tasks required to finish the job. Parallels in the experiences of the competitive athlete and the business person who excels are important to recognize. And it is equally important to recognize that the discipline of letting go of counterproductive but very normal human responses, such as worry and doubt in the face of a profound challenge, is a powerful differentiating feature between those who can deliver and those who can't. It is this, the judgmental response, that we learn to let go of in personal relations. By learning to let go we discover not that judgment is wrong—on the contrary!—but that the ability not to judge opens up new doors of communication between ourselves and the important people in our lives. And it provides us with the material to form our judgments with a wider than ordinary perspective.

Whether the challenge is successfully negotiating a difficult contract or meeting a tight deadline for the submission of an annual report, the peak performance state can be your greatest asset. For the graduate of Peak Performance Training, stress becomes a positive force, similar to the way tough competition becomes a positive force for the athletic champion. Armed with the skills of the peak performer, the ability to let go under pressure, tight deadlines and tough negotiations cause you to reach deeply into your own reserve of hidden resources to find the very best in yourself. Letting go is your key for putting into motion all the peak performance skills you've learned.

Personal: In conflicts with a friend, a lover, a mate, or a family member, stress is frequently high, the stakes being emotional pain or pleasure. In such situations, the threat of emotional pain is generally manifest in physical tension, not unlike most people's response to a threat to physical well-being. In this state of tension, we tend to take a defensive posture, making it all but impossible to hear the other person's side of the story. Hearing your loved one's side of the story, though difficult in the midst of an argument, is absolutely essential for solving personal conflicts. Without that input, there can be no change in a personal relationship, and without change there is no resolution of personal conflicts.

When faced with high stress in personal conflicts, it is not possible to remain cool, calm, and in control at all times. Nor do I believe such a goal would be worth achieving. Nevertheless, the ability to relax and let go, for even brief periods during a personal confrontation, is essential. Use the skills of letting go to let yourself hear the other person's viewpoint without judging it. Then give yourself time to think about not only what that information means to that person but what it means to you and your relationship with him or her.

In psychology, learning to *let go* of one's quite human reflex to judge other people is an essential skill that every therapist must master. I have always felt that much might be gained by passing this skill on to the patient, rather than making it the exclusive property of the therapist.

A gentle reminder here: the letting-go lesson provides you with skills that should *not* be taken out of context from the other five lessons of this training program. Understanding the sources of your greatest volition, establishing a plan for achieving success through goal-setting, developing the ability to relax at will, learning mental rehearsal, and maintaining athletic poise, though separate lessons, are all integral steps for learning to let go.

THE GYM OF THE FUTURE

Wedding Psychology and

High Technology in the

Quest for Peak Performance

> The committed athlete of the future will be able to achieve peak performance only through the use of a comprehensive mental *and* physical training program.
>
> Marilyn King
> Olympic pentathlete

The technology for the gym of the future is already here. We are at that point in history when, rather than creating a technology for the years to come, we are catching up with the present. The technology for our gym comes from a variety of sources. From the space program come not only computer technology but also neurophysiological programming, based on principles developed in flight simulation and psychic self-regulation training; from education come techniques for enhancing and accelerating learning by utilizing the highly receptive states of consciousness we enter during sleep and meditation; from medicine come visualization and biofeedback training to induce optimal physical and mental conditioning; from the computer industry comes the practice of visual stimulation to trigger muscular reflexes in an artificial environment; from the field of biomechanical analysis comes the ability to plot every movement of the body and analyze the data for optimal efficiency and power.

During the coming decade, programs such as those described in this book will be built into gym programs that will be available to both the recreational and competitive athlete. But instead of relying on the written word, the gym of the future will present program guidance through the miracles of the computer age.

On joining the gym in the year 1994, you will be issued a membership card about the size of an ordinary credit card. Encased in the card will be magnetic material that stores a record of your physical and mental condition. (The technology for this is already in use today in the form of medical cards that contain complete records of individual health histories. Also, the U.S. Army has a dog-tag chip that holds all vital statistics and personnel records for each soldier, records that are electronically updated whenever such information changes.)

As you begin your training program at the gym of the future, you will enter a consultation booth where your membership card is fed into a slot. A screen (not unlike those now in use at automatic banking machines) will flash on. As in Lesson 1 of this book, you will be guided through a list of questions and mental exercises that help you to identify activities and experiences with high volitional impact in your life. You will then be given a visualization program for intensifying your volition in your chosen sports activity. This program will then be recorded on the membership card for future reference, and it will be updated from time to time as you progress through the training program.

When you leave the consultation booth, an assistant will apply several round adhesive patches, each about an inch in diameter, to various parts of your body. These will be wireless electrodes (similar to those physicians now use in doing electroencephalograms). Their purpose will be to monitor your heart and respiration rates, galvanic skin response, muscle tension, brain waves, and even the pH factor of your sweat. This data will be fed into a computer, and the results will be printed on your membership card at each step of the training session.

There will be exercise machines, many of which resemble those now found in a Nautilus-type gym—except that the new generation of machines will be equipped with video screens. As you approach a machine, you will insert your membership card and take the appropriate position for working out. On the video screen will appear a graphic representation of the activity you are engaged in, showing your movements in relation to an ideal movement pattern that is appropriate for your relative condition. Thanks to data encoded on your membership card and collected by the electrodes taped to your body, the machine will be automatically programmed, making changes every second or two to provide the optimal workout relative to your changing mental and physical condition. In addition to providing the physical workout, the video screen will simultaneously feed you a visualization exercise to stimulate optimal mental conditioning.

As you look around, you will see that the machines available in this gym are not limited to weight training; there are also "sports simulators." For example, if you are a skier, you will be able to stand on a track before a large video screen, strap your feet into simulated ski bindings, and grasp the handles of two simulated ski poles. When you press a trigger on one of the poles, the video screen will come on, providing a motion picture of a downhill run tailored to your present skill level and showing you exactly how you would look as you skied a real hill. The clamps holding your feet will rise, fall, and twist, as will the ski poles, to simulate the terrain that is flashed on the screen. Your corresponding movements will be reflected in the changing of the picture on the screen, providing the complete experience of an actual run. (Engineers presently experimenting with this technology tell us that even such details as the sound and feel of the wind can be simulated!)

The technology for sports simulators began with the flight simulators developed at NASA and utilized by commercial airline companies to train their pilots. In 1982, at the International Racquet Sports Association convention in Las Vegas, prototypes of sports simulators were exhibited, and it was announced that a major computer manufacturer had joined forces with the leading manufacturer of exercise equipment to develop this technology further.

Throughout your workout at the gym of the future, you will be presented with randomly selected sports encounters designed to challenge poise. If, for example, you are a competitive runner, you might work out on a simulator and see an image of runner after runner passing you on the video screen. If your confidence wanes at this point, revealing that you are discouraged, instructions reminding you of how to regain poise will be flashed on the screen.

At the end of your training session, you will return to the consultation booth. You will insert your card into a slot and then be presented with a number of choices. For example, you might choose to see a graphic representation of your performance from your last workout on any one of the machines— on the screen you would see a detailed representation of yourself performing, with an overlay of how you would look if performing *optimally.* You would be able to control the picture for instant replays or stop action, allowing you to study and visualize what you needed to do to improve your performance.

The kind of computer analysis employed in this will be a product of the science of computer analysis for athletic performance, already being employed in sophisticated sports laboratories. For example, in 1980, American physicist Rocco Rettito used a computer to analyze hundreds of films of athletes in the hammer-throw competition. The key factors he discovered were the angle at which the athlete leans as he builds momentum for the release and the number of times he whirls prior to letting go. He found that Americans leaned backward and spun three times, while the Soviets and East Germans, who threw the hammer up to ten meters farther in competition than American athletes did, leaned *forward* and spun *four* times.

Another choice you might have at the gym of the future is to see a graphic presentation of your progress: You might push a button in the consultation booth and be presented with a graphic layout on the screen of your goals, showing where you had started, where you wanted to go, and which goals you have already completed. The goals graph would include metabolic changes such as aerobic conditioning, muscle bulk, and reflex responses, and might even contain a report on how you were improving in the self-regulation of brain waves (athletic poise) in challenging situations.

Before leaving the booth, you will be given a number of visualizations to work on before your next workout, visualizations designed to preprogram your mind for the next step of your training.

In addition to the machinery available to optimize use of training time in the gym of the future, you will find that sports psychologists are available. These psychologists will have been trained in testing for performance "blocks" and in prescribing programs to help athletes overcome impediments to their success. Techniques for resolving obstacles to succeeding might include biofeedback and hypnosis as well as the relaxation and visualization training that you have already learned in this book.

As we play with our visions of the future, it is important to understand that we are not simply toying with fantasies. Everything described in this section is already in the development stage or is actually being employed on a regular basis in the training of athletes. Although considerable work remains to be done, especially in the creation of effective sports simulators, the greatest task in realizing the gym of the future is that of bringing the separate technologies together under one roof and orchestrating them as described here.

We are at a juncture in history that is something like that time in the nineteenth century when the railroad represented a brand-new technology. For those of us in the sports world, the tracks have already been laid for a new era in athletic training, one that will assist us in setting new records in human achievement. And, for the recreational athlete, the gym of the future promises personal satisfactions that are presently available only to superathletes. But no one need wait for supportive technology to enjoy the benefits of Peak Performance Training. The future is *now,* as realized through your own efforts to follow the Peak Performance Training Program presented in this book.

You hold in your hands the building blocks for the gym of the future. And for you there is no need to wait for the supporting technology that will undoubtedly come. For you the gym of the future is already a reality.

References

Ali, Muhammad, with Durham, Richard. *The Greatest*. New York: Random House, 1975.

Andrews, Valerie. *The Psychic Power of Running*. New York: Ballentine Books, 1978.

Assagioli, Roberto. *Psychosynthesis*. New York: Simon and Schuster, 1968.

Bannister, Roger. *The Four-Minute Mile*. London, 1956.

Basmajian, John. *Muscles Alive: Their Functions Revealed by Electromyography*. Baltimore: Williams and Wilkins, 1962.

Benson, Herbert. *The Mind/Body Effect*. New York: Simon and Schuster, 1979.

Blakeslee, T. R. *The Right Brain*. New York: Anchor Press, 1980.

Block, Alex B. *The Legend of Bruce Lee*. New York: Dell, 1974.

Brodie, John, and Houston, James D. *Open Field*. New York: Bantam, 1974.

Brown, Barbara. *Stress and the Art of Biofeedback*. New York: Harper and Row, 1977.

Butt, Dorcas Susan. *The Psychology of Sport*. New York: Van Nostrand Reinhold, 1976.

Cade, C. M., and Coxhead, N. *The Awakened Mind*. New York: Dell, 1979.

Cooper, Kenneth. *The Aerobics Way*. New York: Evans, 1977.

Cooper, Linn F., and Erickson, Milton H. *Time Distortion in Hypnosis*. Baltimore: Williams and Wilkins, 1954.

Cousy, Bob, with Al Hirshberg. *Basketball Is My Life*. Englewood Cliffs, N.J.: Prentice-Hall, 1958.

DeVore, Steven, and DeVore, Greggory R., with Michaelson, Mike. *SyberVision: Muscle Memory Programming*. Chicago: Chicago Review Press, 1981.

Farrelly, Midget, with McGregor, C. *The Surfing Life*. New York: Arco, 1967.

Feldenkrais, M. *The Elusive Obvious*. Cupertino, Calif.: Meta Publications, 1981.

Ferguson, Marilyn. *The Brain Revolution*. New York: Taplinger, 1973.

Fixx, James. *The Complete Book of Running.* New York: Random House, 1977.

Gaines, Charles, and Butler, George. *Pumping Iron.* New York: Simon and Schuster, 1974.

Gallwey, Timothy. *The Inner Game of Tennis.* New York: Random House, 1974.

Ghiselin, Brewster, ed. *The Creative Process.* New York: New American Library, 1955.

Glasser, William. *Positive Addiction.* New York: Harper and Row, 1976.

Green, Elmer, and Green, Alyce. *Beyond Biofeedback.* New York: Dial Press, 1977.

Greenspan, Bud, and Greenspan, C. P. *Numero Uno.* New York: Signet Books, 1982.

Guyton, Arthur C. *Physiology of the Human Body.* Philadelphia: W. B. Saunders Company, 1979.

Hall, Evelyn, and Hardy, Charles. "Using the Right Brain in Sports." In *New Path to Sport Learning* (transcripts of symposium). Coaching Association of Canada. Ottawa: Canada, 1982.

Harris, T. G. "Why Pros Meditate." *Psychology Today,* October 1975, p. 4.

Hendricks, Gay, and Carlson, J. *The Centered Athlete.* Englewood Cliffs, N.J.: Prentice-Hall, 1982.

Herrigel, Eugen. *Zen in the Art of Archery.* New York: Pantheon, 1953.

Hickman, James L. "How to Elicit Supernormal Capabilities in Athletes." In *Coach, Athlete, and the Sport Psychologist,* edited by Peter Klavora and Juri V. Daniel. Toronto, Canada: University of Toronto School of Physical and Health Education, 1979.

Hunter, Catfish, with George Vass. "The Game I'll Never Forget." *Baseball Digest,* June 1973, pp. 35–37.

Huntley, Noel. *Superhuman: Man's Ultimate Physical and Spiritual Abilities.* Los Angeles: Prescience Publications, 1981.

Huxley, Aldous. *The Perennial Philosophy.* New York: Harper and Row, 1945.

Hyams, Joe. *Zen in the Martial Arts.* Los Angeles: J. P. Tarcher, 1979.

James, William. *The Energies of Man.* New York: Moffat, Yard, 1908.

Jenner, Bruce. *Decathlon Challenge.* Englewood Cliffs, N.J.: Prentice-Hall, 1977.

Jerome, John. *The Sweet Spot in Time.* New York: Avon, 1982.

REFERENCES

Kauss, David R. *Peak Performance*. New York: Spectrum Books, 1980.

Kellner, Stan, *Taking It to the Limit*. Stan Kellner, P.O. Box 134, East Setauket, New York, 11733: 1979.

King, Billie Jean, with Chapin, K. *Billie Jean*. New York: Harper and Row, 1974.

Kloboucher, Jim. *Tarkenton*. New York: Harper and Row, 1976.

Krippner, Stanley. *Human Possibilities*. New York: Anchor, 1980.

Leonard, George. *The Ultimate Athlete*. New York: Viking, 1975.

Loehr, James E. "The Ideal Performance State." *Science Periodical on Research and Technology in Sport*. Canada: Government of Canada, BU-1, January 1983.

Lucas, John. "Anomalies of Human Physical Achievement." *Canadian Journal of History of Sport*, December 1977, pp. 231–247.

Murphy, Michael. *The Psychic Side of Sports*. New York: Addison Wesley, 1978.

Murphy, Michael, and Brodie, John. "I Experience a Kind of Clarity." *Intellectual Digest*, January 1973, pp. 19–22.

Namath, Joe, with Schaap, D. *I Can't Wait Until Tomorrow—'Cause I Get Better-Looking Every Day*. New York: Random House, 1969.

Nideffer, R. M. *The Inner Athlete*. New York: Crowell, 1976.

Pele, with Fish, R. L. *My Life and the Beautiful Game*. Garden City, New York: Doubleday, 1977.

Pulos, Lee. "Self-Hypnosis and Think Training with Athletes." In *Coach, Athlete, and the Sport Psychologist*, edited by Peter Klavora and Juri V. Daniel. Champaign, Illinois: Human Kinetics Publishers, 1979.

Raiport, Gregory, interviewed by MacKenzie MacKay. "The Soviets' Secret Weapon . . . Hockey Psychology." Action Sports *Hockey*, January 1980.

Ravizza, Kenneth. "A Study of the Peak Experience in Sport." Ph.D. dissertation, University of Southern California, 1973.

Rico, G. L. *Writing the Natural Way*. Los Angeles: J. P. Tarcher, 1983.

Rushall, Brent. *Psyching in Sport*. London: Pelham Books, 1979.

Russell, Bill. *Second Wind*. New York: Random House, 1979.

Rychta, Taduesz. "Psychology of Training: Philosophical Choices." Mental Training for Coaches and Athletes, Sport in Perspective, Inc. (transcripts of symposium). Ottawa, Canada: Coaching Association of Canada, 1982.

Schwarz, Jack. *Voluntary Controls*. New York: Dutton, 1978.

Schwarzenegger, Arnold. *Arnold: The Education of a Body-builder.* New York: Simon and Schuster, 1977.

Sheehan, George. *Running and Being.* New York: Simon and Schuster, 1978.

Simonton, Carl, and Simonton, Stephanie. *Getting Well Again.* Los Angeles: J. P. Tarcher, 1978.

Slusher, Howard. *Man, Sport and Existence.* Philadelphia: Lea and Febiger, 1967.

Sperling, Dan. "The Myth of the Natural Athlete." *Success,* February 1982, pp. 23–25.

Sport in Perspective, Inc. *Mental Training for Coaches and Athletes* (transcripts of symposium). Ottawa, Canada: Coaching Association of Canada, 1982.

Suinn, Richard M. "Body Thinking: Psychology for Olympic Champs." *Psychology Today,* July 1976.

Suzuki, D. T. *Zen Buddhism.* Edited by William Barrett. New York: Anchor Books, 1956.

Tutko, Thomas. *Sports Psyching: Playing Your Best Game All of the Time.* Los Angeles: J. P. Tarcher, 1976.

Unestahl, Lars-Eric. "Hypnotic Preparation of Athletes." Paper published at the Department of Sport Psychology, Orebro University, Sweden, June 1979.

Vandell, R. A., Davis, R. A., and Clugston, H. A. "The Function of Mental Practice in the Acquisition of Motor Skills." *Journal of General Psychology,* October 1943, pp. 243–250.

Weitzberg, N. E., and Altman, K. P. "Enhancing Sport Performance." Paper presented to the Convention of the California State Psychological Association, 1978.

Werthman, Michael. *Self-Psyching: 35 Proven Techniques for Overcoming Common Psychological Problems.* Los Angeles: J. P. Tarcher, 1978.

Wilson, V. E., and Bird, E. I. "Understanding Self-Regulation Training in Sport." *Science Periodical on Research and Technology in Sport,* October 1982.

Winter, Bud. *Relax and Win.* La Jolla, Calif.: A. S. Barnes and Co., 1981.

Suggested Reading

Beyond Biofeedback, by Elmer Green and Alyce Green (New York, Dial Press, 1977).

Elmer and Alyce Green, two of the leading biofeedback researchers in the world, have made a tremendous contribution to the literature of self-regulation training. In this book the Greens have established a foundation for understanding the crucial connection between mind and body. Working at one of our country's most prestigious institutions, the Menninger Foundation, the Greens have been in the vanguard of American research in mind-body dynamics, and their work constitutes an invaluable addition to those athletes and coaches interested in both in-depth and broader applications of these relatively new fields of scientific endeavor. The Greens have also amply demonstrated that a solid body of important work on self-regulation has been ongoing in the United States and that this research has by no means been limited to the U.S.S.R. and East Germany. This fact, their work, and the work of other American researchers, points to the fact that although we have had important work available—work that in most respects is at least equal to that of the Soviets—we have simply not translated it to our athletes and coaches in forms that are usable. This book is *must* reading for everyone wanting to understand the psychophysiological basis for Peak Performance Training, biofeedback, and other self-regulation techniques.

Coach, Athlete, and the Sports Psychologist, edited by Peter Klavora and Juri V. Daniel (University of Toronto School of Physical and Health Education, Toronto, Canada, 1976).

For those interested in the burgeoning field of sports psychology and a more in-depth look at the major contributions that psychology has made to peak performance in sports, this book is an excellent place to begin. Klavora and Daniel have here compiled a fine collection of articles by leading figures in sports and sports psychology, and have specifically addressed the issue of the emotional factors involved in high-level performance. This book is an example of the kind of solid work being done and constitutes an antidote to a great deal of the "pop psychology" and watered-down faddish approaches to mental training so frequently encountered. I recommend this book highly to those still wondering what role the sport psychologist plays in the lives of accomplished athletes and coaches.

Golf My Way, by Jack Nicklaus (New York, Simon and Schuster, 1974).

Arguably golf's greatest performer, and one of America's most successful businessmen, Jack Nicklaus is a study in mental and physical prowess at the highest level. His unequivocal support of mental preparation as the single most critical element in peak performance makes him an especially useful case study. Nicklaus says, "I never hit a shot, not even in practice, without having a very clear, in-focus picture of it in my head." Whether you take Nicklaus's golf instruction literally or as a metaphor for peak performance in general, his book offers a solid look at one of our most intelligent and sophisticated athletes.

Peak Performance (cassette program), by Charles Garfield (published by Performance Sciences, 106 Evergreen Lane, Berkeley, CA 94705).

An audiotape-book program developed specifically for those interested in extending the principles of peak performance to other areas of life, particularly career excellence. This program includes tape-recorded interviews with peak performers, including Olympic and world-class athletes, senior business executives, and high performing professionals in a variety of fields.

Second Wind, by Bill Russell (New York, Random House, 1979).

The single best biographical account of the importance of mental training in sport. Russell's compelling account of how he used his mind as an inner laboratory for improving his performance is classic and extremely informative. Russell's description of his lifelong practice of mental rehearsal and its prominent role in transforming him from an average high school athlete to a dominant force in the NBA should be mandatory reading for anyone embarking on a serious peak performance training program.

Seeing with the Mind's Eye, by Mike Samuels and Nancy Samuels (New York, Random House, 1975).

Without question my favorite book on imagery and visualization, *Seeing with the Mind's Eye* contains a great deal of practical information grounded in solid research on the use of visualization and mental rehearsal. Not only do the Samuelses present practical approaches but they also provide a comprehensive framework for understanding the connection between the ability to visualize and mentally rehearse and great achievement in all human endeavors. Any serious competitive or recreational athlete will find the potential of visualization and mental rehearsal clearly outlined in this book. Once you have read the book, it becomes impossible to ignore the mental side of sport and its key role in peak performance.

Science Periodical on Research and Technology in Sport (The Coaching Association of Canada, Ottawa, Canada).

This monthly newsletter/journal covers some of the most practical and important information on sports training, the intended audience being those committed to athletics. Reporting on the latest developments in Peak Performance Training in sport—mental training, physical training, nutrition, coaching issues, and so forth—this source is most useful to those who want state-of-the-art information quickly. Although it is a highly condensed journal, I have rarely been disappointed in its contents—the quality of the monthly issues is extremely high.

The Jim Plunkett Story, by Jim Plunkett and Dave Newhouse (New York, Arbor House, 1976).

One of the signs of the peak performer is the ability to overcome adversity, the inevitable rough times. Jim Plunkett's adversity-riddled, rags to riches career (born to poor, blind, Mexican-American parents, he led Stanford University to a Rose Bowl victory, won the Heisman Trophy, and was selected NFL rookie of the year) and his inspiring comeback from the professional football junkyard to two Superbowl triumphs, is a lesson in commitment and perseverence fit to instruct competitive and recreational athletes alike.

The Peak Performance Center, located at 106 Evergreen Lane in Berkeley, California, 94705, has, since its founding in 1979, functioned as an international clearing house for individuals and organizations committed to achieving peak performance and productivity, and has responded, without charge, to more than 200,000 requests for articles and other information.

Index

Accuracy, in mental imagery, 81, 85
Achievement, high. *See* Peak performance
Actions. *See* Movements
Addiction, positive, 97
Ali, Muhammad, 103–104
Altman, Kerry Paul, 37
Andrews, Valerie, 22–23
Anthropomaximology, 17
Anxiety, 24, 105, 107. *See also* Negative emotions
Apollo space program, 20–21, 66, 129
Assagioli, Roberto, 40
Athletic poise, 155–195. *See also* Psychological readiness
Athletic training. *See* Peak Performance Training Program
Attention. *See* Focus of attention
Attitudes, 24, 37. *See also* Psychological readiness
Autogenic training, 21, 114, 115
  and fight-or-flight response, 102
  repetitive style of presentation, 8
  time required for results, 115
Autogenic Training (exercise), 114–123
Automatic actions, 26, 27, 29, 103. *See also* Letting go
Autonomic functions
  achieving control of, 39
  effects of the mind on, 20, 24
  self-regulation of, 14, 35–36, 91–92; *see also* Self-regulation
  volition and, 36–38

Awakened Mind, The (Cade and Coxhead), 99

Bannister, Roger, 97
Baseball players, 37, 180, 185
Basketball players, 27, 73, 97, 131–132, 133
Bennett, Hal Zina, 125
Benson, Herbert, 125
Beyond Biofeedback (Green and Green), 21, 40
Biofeedback, 8, 14, 20, 35
Biographers, methods used by, 42
Blakeslee, T. R., 98
Blalock, Jane, 99, 185
Body-builders, 23, 81–82, 136
Boxers, 27, 103–104
Brain hemisphere dominance, 124
  during athletic activities, 98–99
  and breathing, 110–111
  left hemisphere, 98–99, 182, 186
  in mental imagery, 142
  during relaxation, 95, 96, 99
  right hemisphere, 97–99, 182, 188
  and sleep, 104–105
Brainstorming, 42–43, 59–60
Breathing, 101
  brain and, 110–111
  diaphragmatic, 106, 110–114, 115
  thoracic, 110–111, 112
Breathing for Peak Performance (exercise), 110–114
Brodie, John, 137
Business. *See* Career/business applications

INDEX